First World War
and Army of Occupation
War Diary
France, Belgium and Germany

3 CAVALRY DIVISION
Divisional Troops
Royal Army Service Corps
Divisional Auxiliary Horse Transport Company (576
Company A.S.C.)
24 January 1916 - 16 May 1919

WO95/1151/1

The Naval & Military Press Ltd
www.nmarchive.com
Published in association with The National Archives

Published by

The Naval & Military Press Ltd

Unit 10 Ridgewood Industrial Park,

Uckfield, East Sussex,

TN22 5QE England

Tel: +44 (0) 1825 749494

www.naval-military-press.com

www.nmarchive.com

This diary has been reprinted in facsimile from the original. Any imperfections are inevitably reproduced and the quality may fall short of modern type and cartographic standards.

© Crown Copyright
Images reproduced by permission of The National Archives, London, England, 2015.

Contents

Document type	Place/Title	Date From	Date To
Heading	B.E.F. France & Flanders. 3 Cavalry Div. Troops. 3 Cavalry Div Auxiliary Horse Transport Coy. (576 Coy A.S.C.) 1916 Jan To 1919 May. 3 Cav Div Ammn Park. (76 Coy A.S.C.) 1915 Feb To 1917 Oct.		
Heading	WO95/1151/1		
Heading	No. 3. Cav Div. Aux Horse Tpt Coy. 1916 Jan-1919 May. (576 Coy ASC)		
Heading	War Diary of the 3rd Cavalry Divisional Auxiliary Horse Transport Co., A.S.C. 24th January to 29th February, 1916 to April 1919		
War Diary	Fruges	24/01/1916	21/06/1916
War Diary	Le Boisle	22/06/1916	22/06/1916
War Diary	Abbeville	23/06/1916	25/06/1916
War Diary	Argoeuvres	26/06/1916	26/06/1916
War Diary	Corbie	27/06/1916	10/07/1916
War Diary	Bois De Taille (South)	11/07/1916	31/07/1916
War Diary	Nr Etinehem	01/08/1916	21/08/1916
War Diary	Nr Meaulte	22/08/1916	13/09/1916
War Diary	Daours	14/09/1916	05/11/1916
War Diary	Beaurainville	06/11/1916	25/11/1916
War Diary	St. Denoeux	26/11/1916	21/12/1916
War Diary	Beaurainville	22/12/1916	23/01/1917
War Diary	Lespinoy	24/01/1917	03/03/1917
War Diary	St. Denoeux	04/03/1917	07/04/1917
War Diary	Monchel	08/04/1917	08/04/1917
War Diary	Boubers-Sur-Canche	09/04/1917	10/04/1917
War Diary	Etree Wamin	11/04/1917	11/04/1917
War Diary	Fosseux	12/04/1917	12/04/1917
War Diary	Etree Wamin	13/04/1917	20/04/1917
War Diary	Regnauville	21/04/1917	13/05/1917
War Diary	Wavans	14/05/1917	14/05/1917
War Diary	Talmas	15/05/1917	15/05/1917
War Diary	Querrieu	16/05/1917	17/05/1917
War Diary	La Motte	18/05/1917	19/05/1917
War Diary	Courcelles	20/05/1917	03/07/1917
War Diary	Flamicourt	04/07/1917	04/07/1917
War Diary	Treux	05/07/1917	05/07/1917
War Diary	Doullens	06/07/1917	06/07/1917
War Diary	Sains	07/07/1917	07/07/1917
War Diary	Pernes	08/07/1917	16/07/1917
War Diary	Busnes	17/07/1917	31/08/1917
Heading	War Diary of September 1917 3rd Cav. Div. Aux. Hrs		
War Diary	Busnes	01/09/1917	30/09/1917
Heading	War Diary of 3rd Cavalry Divl. A.H.J.C October, 1917		
War Diary	Busnes	01/10/1917	17/10/1917
War Diary	Pernes	18/10/1917	23/10/1917
War Diary	Domart	24/10/1917	31/10/1917
Heading	War Diary of 3 Cavalry Div. Aux. H. J. Co. for November 1917 Vol 22		
War Diary	Domart	01/11/1917	18/11/1917

War Diary	Etinehem	19/11/1917	23/11/1917
War Diary	Beauquesne	24/11/1917	30/11/1917
War Diary	Corbie	01/12/1917	21/12/1917
War Diary	Domart	22/12/1917	31/12/1917
War Diary	Field	01/01/1918	31/08/1918
War Diary	Willencourt	01/09/1918	17/09/1918
War Diary	Cherienne	18/09/1918	26/09/1918
War Diary	Lens II Albert Sheet 62. C. H.5.C. Central	27/09/1918	30/09/1918
War Diary	Sheet 62. C. H.5.C. Central	01/10/1918	10/10/1918
War Diary	Sheet 62. C. K. 21. C. Central	11/10/1918	14/10/1918
War Diary	U.10.B.2.8.	15/10/1918	21/10/1918
War Diary	Sheet 57 C U.10 B. 2. 8	21/10/1918	31/10/1918
War Diary	U.10 B. 2. 8	01/11/1918	12/11/1918
War Diary	Wattiesart	13/11/1918	13/11/1918
War Diary	Bury	14/11/1918	19/11/1918
War Diary	Englien	20/11/1918	21/11/1918
War Diary	Waterloo	22/11/1918	22/11/1918
War Diary	Pernez	23/11/1918	24/11/1918
War Diary	Odenge	25/11/1918	30/11/1918
Heading	Auxiliary Horse Transport Coy 3rd Cav. Div War Diary December 1918		
War Diary	Odenge Nr Perwez	01/12/1918	13/12/1918
War Diary	Odenge	14/12/1918	15/12/1918
War Diary	Bienwart	16/12/1918	16/12/1918
War Diary	Modave	17/12/1918	31/12/1918
Heading	Auxiliary Horse Transport Company. 3rd Cavalry Division. January 1919 Vol 36		
War Diary	Modave	01/01/1919	28/02/1919
War Diary	Modave S of Huy	01/03/1919	06/03/1919
War Diary	Clermont Nr Engis	07/03/1919	15/03/1919
War Diary	Clermont	16/03/1919	09/04/1919
War Diary	Jemmeppe	10/04/1919	16/05/1919
War Diary	Jemmeppe	01/05/1919	16/05/1919

B.E.F. FRANCE & FLANDERS.

3 CAVALRY DIV. TROOPS.

3 CAVALRY DIV AUXILIARY
HORSE TRANSPORT COY.
(576 COY A.S.C.)
1916 JAN TO 1919 MAY.

3 CAV DIV AMMN PARK.
(76 COY A.S.C.)
1915 FEB TO 1917 OCT.

B.E.F. FRANCE & FLANDERS.
3 CAVALRY DIV. TROOPS.
3 CAVALRY DIV AUXILIARY
HORSE TRANSPORT COY.
(576 COY A.S.C.)
1916 JAN TO 1919 MAY.
3 CAV DIV AMMN PARK.
(76 COY A.S.C.)
1915 FEB TO 1917 OCT.

1151

3rd CAV DIV Troops

NO. 3. CAV DIV.
AUX HORSE TPT COY.
1916 JAN - 1919 MAY.

(576 Coy ASC)

NO Box

WAR DIARY of the

3rd CAVALRY DIVISIONAL AUXILIARY HORSE TRANSPORT CO., A.S.C.

24th January to 29th February, 1916.   50   April 1919

WAR DIARY
INTELLIGENCE SUMMARY
(Erase heading not required.)

Army Form C. 2118

Instructions regarding War Diaries and Intelligence Summaries are contained in F.S. Regs., Part II. and the Staff Manual respectively. Title Pages will be prepared in manuscript.

Place	Date	Hour	Summary of Events and Information	Remarks and references to Appendices
FRUGES	24-1-16		Railhead MONTREUIL Refilling Point Supply Dump. Rue de STOMER FRUGES Billets FRUGES Lieut. C.G.R WELLER joined from leave and took over command of the Company	
do	25-1-16		R.H, R.P, & B. same as 24-1-16	
do	26-1-16		see 25-1-16.	
do	27-1-16		R.H R.P & B same as 24-1-16 2 men sent to Hospital at FRUGES	
do	28-1-16		R.H. R.P. & B same as 24-1-16 Act. Corpl HOSGOOD reverted to permanent rank (Driver) 2 men sent to Hospital at FRUGES 2 horses destroyed on account of severe injuries received C.J.R.Shelly. Lieut O.C. 3rd (Can) ir. Divc H.T. Coy	

WAR DIARY
of
INTELLIGENCE SUMMARY

(Erase heading not required.)

Army Form C. 2118

Place	Date	Hour	Summary of Events and Information	Remarks and references to Appendices
FRUGES	29-1-16		Railhead, MONTREUIL. Refilling Point, Supply Dump Rue de ST OMER FRUGES. Billets FRUGES.	
do	30-1-16		Same as 29-1-16.	
do	31-1-16		Same as 29-1-16.	
do	1-2-16		Same as 29-1-16.	
do	2-2-16		R.H., R.P. & D. same as 29-1-16. 2 men returned from Hospital at FRUGES.	
do	3-2-16		R.H. R.P. & B. same as 29-1-16.	
do	4-2-16		Same as 29-1-16.	
do	5-2-16		R.H. R.P.+B. Same as 29-1-16. Inspection in Marching order by O.C. A.S.C. no complaints. One Driver reported from B.H.T.D. C/Rholley Lieut. O.C. 3rd Cav. Div Ammoc H.T. Coy.	

WAR DIARY
or
INTELLIGENCE SUMMARY
(Erase heading not required.)

Army Form C. 2118

Place	Date	Hour	Summary of Events and Information	Remarks and references to Appendices
FRUGES	6-2-16		Railhead MONTREUIL. Refilling point Supply dump. Rue de STOMER FRUGES. Billets FRUGES.	
do	7-2-16		R.H, R.P, & B, same as 6-2-16. One Corporal reported from Base. One waggon lent for the day to C.F.A.	
do	8-2-16		R.H, R.P, B. same as 6-2-16. Received wire to say that waggon with "C" Battery R.H.A. had broken down.	
do	9-2-16		R.H, R.P, & B same as 6-2-16. One Man received from Hospital. 5 Drivers advanced to 4th Rate of Corps Pay. Sent 1 waggon to "C" Battery R.H.A. to replace one damaged.	
do	10-2-16		R.H, R.P & B same as 6-2-16. Sent 1 waggon to "G" Battery R.H.A. to replace one damaged and Intimation received that waggon with 3rd D.G's had been sent to Base.	

E.W. Ogilby Lieut.
O.C. 3rd Cav Div Amm. H.T. Coy.

WAR DIARY
INTELLIGENCE SUMMARY

Army Form C. 2118

Place	Date	Hour	Summary of Events and Information	Remarks and references to Appendices
FRUGES.	11-2-16		Railhead MONTREUIL Refilling point Supply dump Rue de STOMER FRUGES Billets FRUGES.	
do	12-2-16		One Driver transferred to 81 Coy A.S.C. (H.Q.C. 3rd C.D) R.H. R.P. & B. as 11-2-16. 3 waggons, teams & Drivers sent to H.Q. 4th Brigade.	
do	13-2-16		R.H. R.S. & B. as 11-2-16. 1 L.D. horse "G" Battery R.H.A. destroyed. 1 waggon L.P. —— condemned about 1-2-16.	
do	14-2-16		R.H. R.P. & B. as 14-2-16. Tpr. reported from N. Somerset Yeomanry. 1 L.D. horse to "G" Battery	
do	15-2-16		R.H. R.P. & B. as 11-2-16. One man admitted, and one man returned from Hospital.	

A.J. Riddley Lieut.
3rd (Cav.) Div Divc H.T. Coy

Army Form C. 2118

WAR DIARY
INTELLIGENCE SUMMARY
(Erase heading not required.)

Place	Date	Hour	Summary of Events and Information	Remarks and references to Appendices
FRUGES	16-2-16		Railhead MONTREUIL. Refilling point Supply dump Rue de STOMER FRUGES. Billets FRUGES.	
do	17-2-16		R.A. RPqB as 16-2-16. 1 Driver to R.H.T.D.	
do	18-2-16		R.A. RPqB as 16-2-16. Lce Cpl from R.A.M.C. sanitary section reported. 3 horses returned from H.Q. 4th Brigade, sent out on 12th inst.	
do	19-2-16		R.A. RPqB. as 16-2-16. 1 Driver reported from B.H.T.D.	
do	20-2-16		R.A. RP.B. as 16-2-16. 1 Driver to hospital.	

Campbell Lieut.
O.C. 3rd (Car D) w Cwoc. H.T. Coy.

Army Form C. 2118

WAR DIARY
INTELLIGENCE SUMMARY
(Erase heading not required.)

Place	Date	Hour	Summary of Events and Information	Remarks and references to Appendices
FRUGES	21-2-16		Railhead MONTREUIL. Refilling point, Supply dump Rue de STOMER FRUGES. Billets FRUGES. 2 LD horses Evacuated to Vety Mobile station.	
do	22-2-16		R.H. R.P. & B. as 21-2-16. 3 G.S. waggons received from D.O Calais. 1 Driver to Hospital. 1 — from Hospital.	
do	23-2-16		R.H. R.P. & B. as 21-2-16. 2 Drivers to Hospital.	
do	24-2-16		R.H. R.P. & B. as 21-2-16. Received notice that all leave stopped until further orders, except under special circumstances. 1 Driver from Hospital.	

CPWheller Lieut.
O.C. 3rd Cav. Div. Auxe H.T. Coy.

WAR DIARY
or
INTELLIGENCE SUMMARY

(Erase heading not required.)

Army Form C. 2118

Place	Date	Hour	Summary of Events and Information	Remarks and references to Appendices
FRUGES	25-2-16		Railhead MONTREUIL. Refilling point Supply dump Rue de St OMER. FRUGES. Billets FRUGES. Horses inspected by O.C. A.S.C. 3rd Cav.D. at 11 a.m. (Cradick:- slight improvement in condition of horses). Court of Enquiry held to ascertain cause of injury to Sgt. Turner	
do	26-2-16		R.H. RP+B ao 25-2-16. 2 Drivers admitted to Hospital ____ received from ____	
do	27-2-16		R.H. RP+B ao 25-2-16 2 Drivers received from Hospital	
do	28-2-16		R.H. RP+B ao 25-2-16 Received all iron rations in place of fresh meat	

CJ Morlet Lieut
O.C. 3rd Cav. Div. Aux. H.T. Coy

WAR DIARY / INTELLIGENCE SUMMARY

Army Form C. 2118

Place	Date	Hour	Summary of Events and Information	Remarks and references to Appendices
FRUGES.	29-2-16		Railhead MONTREUIL. Refilling point Supply Dump Rue de ST OMER. FRUGES. Billets FRUGES.	
do	1-3-16		1 Driver from Hospital. R.H. RP&B. ao 29-2-16. Inspected first Section of Coy. Inspected horses, harness & waggon with "C" Bakery R.H.A.	
do	2-3-16		R.H. RP&B as 29-2-16. 1 Sgt and 1 L/Cpl reports from 1st A.T.D 1 man received from Hospital 1 G.S. waggon received from O.O. Calais	
do	3-3-16		R.H. RP&B. ao 29-2-16. Inspected Billets.	
do	4-3-16		R.H. RP&B. ao 29-2-16.	

CAPholley Lieut.
O.C. 3rd Cav. Div. Auxr. H.T. Coy

WAR DIARY
or
INTELLIGENCE SUMMARY

Army Form C. 2118

Place	Date	Hour	Summary of Events and Information	Remarks and references to Appendices
FRUGES.	5-3-16		Railhead MONTREUIL. Refilling point. Supply dump. Rue de ST OMER. FRUGES. Billets FRUGES.	
do	6-3-16		R.H. R.P.+B. as 5-3-16. Inspected No 2 Section of Coy. 1st Cpl to Hospital.	
do	7-3-16		R.H. R.P.+B. as 5-3-16. 2 horses damaged drawing brushwood from HEZECQUES	
do	8-3-16		R.H. R.P.+B. as 5-3-16.	
do	9-3-16		R.H. R.P.+B. as 5-3-16. 1 Driver evacuated to No 22 C.C.S. Court of Inquiry reassembled in re injury to Sgt Turner, to take medical evidence.	

C.P.Challen Lieut.
O.C. 3rd Can Div Amm. A.T. Coy

WAR DIARY
or
INTELLIGENCE SUMMARY
(Erase heading not required.)

Army Form C. 2118

Place	Date	Hour	Summary of Events and Information	Remarks and references to Appendices
FRUGES	10-3-16		Railhead MONTREUIL. Refilling Point Supply Dump Rue de ST OMER. FRUGES. Billets FRUGES.	
do	11-3-16		R.H. R.P. B. as 10-3-16. 1 Sergt. returned from Base Hospital. 1 L.P. waggon evacuated to O.O. Base.	
do	12-3-16		R.H. R.P. & B. as 10-3-16. Inspected kit of whole Company. Wesley Cpl returned from Hospital.	
do	13-3-16		R.H. R.P. & B. as 10-3-16. Evacuated 1 horse to 13 M.V.S. I find the some of the L.P. waggons belonging to the Co. weigh 30 cwt. and are too heavy for the type of horse in the Co.	
do	14-3-16		R.H. R.P. & B. as 10-3-16.	

C.A. Rheller Lieut
O.C. 3rd Cav. Div. Cav. N.T. Coy.

WAR DIARY
or
INTELLIGENCE SUMMARY

(Erase heading not required.)

Army Form C. 2118

Place	Date	Hour	Summary of Events and Information	Remarks and references to Appendices
FRUGES	15-3-16		Railhead MONTREUIL Refilling point Supply Dump Rue de ST OMER FRUGES. Billets FRUGES. 1 Driver sent to Hospital. 1 G/S waggon received from Base. Inspection of all horses by V.O. no skin diseases found.	
do	16-3-16		R.H. R.P. & B. as 15-3-16.	
do	17-3-16		R.H. R.P. & B. as 15-3-16. Inspected 4 horses on Command with 1st Life Guards at RUMILLY. found them in good condition. Also inspected 4 horses on Command with 2nd Life Guards at HUCQUELIERS. Also in good condition	
do	18-3-16		R.H. R.P. & B. as 15-3-16. Billets inspected by Lt. Scudell & S.S.O. Lyons. Inspected N° 3 & N°D. Pr Sections. Farrier Evacuated	

C.P. Norllel Lieut
O.C. 3rd Rev Div Amc Lt. T. Coy

WAR DIARY or INTELLIGENCE SUMMARY

Army Form C. 2118

Place	Date	Hour	Summary of Events and Information	Remarks and references to Appendices
FRUGES.	19-3-16		Railhead MONTREUIL. Refilling Point Supplydump Rue deS? OMER. FRUGES. Billets FRUGES.	
do	20-3-16		RH RP+B as 19-3-16. DR kindly appointed a L/c Cpl with pay as from 2-3-16. 1 S.D. Horse sent to N°. 114 M.V.S.	
do	21-3-16		RH RP+B as 19-3-16 1 Driver transferred to N°. 7. C.F.A.	
do	22-3-16		RH RP+B as 19-3-16.	
do	23-3-16		RH RP+B as 19-3-16. Received notice of inspection by G.O.C. 3rd Cav.Div. to take place on 24th inst.	
do	24-3-16		RH RP+B as 19-3-16.	

C.G.Worthy Lieut.
O.C 3rd Cav.Div. Divn U.T. Coy.

WAR DIARY
INTELLIGENCE SUMMARY

Army Form C. 2118

Place	Date	Hour	Summary of Events and Information	Remarks and references to Appendices
FRUGES	25/3/16		RAILHEAD MONTREUIL. Refilling Point Supply Dump. Rue du STOMER. Billets FRUGES. FRUGES Received 11 L.D. horses + 5 Riders from Base (including 1 Rider for A.d.) G/no A.S.C. 1 Driver evacuated to 22 C.C.S.	
do	26.3.16		R.H RP+B. as 25-3-16	
do	27.3.16		R.H RP+B. as 25-3-16. Inspection in Marching order by G.O.C. 3rd Cav Div. (per Col Featherstonhaugh) 1 Driver received from No 2 C.C.S. 1 Driver evacuated to No 2 C.C.S	
do	28.3.16		R.H RP+B as 25-3-16 1 L.D horse evacuated to No 13 M.V.S. 1 Driver admitted to D.R.S. Accident to waggon + team at TRAMECOURT. Pole + Reins of waggon only, broken. C.J. Plunkett Lieut O/C 3rd Cav Div Amce H.T. Coy	

WAR DIARY
or
INTELLIGENCE SUMMARY
(Erase heading not required.)

Army Form C. 2118

Instructions regarding War Diaries and Intelligence Summaries are contained in F. S. Regs., Part II. and the Staff Manual respectively. Title Pages will be prepared in manuscript.

Place	Date	Hour	Summary of Events and Information	Remarks and references to Appendices
FRUGES	1-4-16		Railhead MONTREUIL Refilling point Supply Depot Rue de ST OMER FRUGES Billets FRUGES.	
do	2-4-16		R.H. R.P. & B. as 1-4-16. 1 Pair horses attached to waggon bolted in Town, knocking down Lamp & damaging house.	
do	3-4-16		R.H. R.P. & B. as 1-4-16. 1 man sent to D.R.S. 2 L.P. waggons evacuated to O.O. Base.	
do	4-4-16		R.H. R.P. & B. as 1-4-16. Medical Inspection by D.A.D.M.S. 6 pairs + 2 teams sent to 7th Brigade for Road making.	
do	5-4-16		R.H. R.P. & B. as 1-4-16. 1 Driver to D.R.S. 2 Lieut Scudell on leave to U.K. T/20946 A/Cpl Blackman R reverted to Driver and sent to Base for discharge. 6 Lead pairs sent to 7th Brigade for Roadmaking. C.P. Moller Lieut. O.C. 3rd Cav Div Aux. H.T. Coy.	

WAR DIARY
or
INTELLIGENCE SUMMARY
(Erase heading not required.)

Army Form C. 2118

Place	Date	Hour	Summary of Events and Information	Remarks and references to Appendices
FRUGES	6-4-16		Railhead MONTREUIL Refilling point Supply Dump Rue de ST OMER. FRUGES. Billets FRUGES. T/24300 L/Cpl Graham Apptd A Cpl with pay. 1 Driver from D R S.	
do	7-4-16		R.H. R.P.& D. as 6-4-16. 1 Driver returned from No 2 C.C.S. 1 Driver received from N.S. Yeomanry. 1 Driver to D.R.S. Inspection of houses for casting by V.O. 2 G/S waggons from B.O. Calais	
do	8-4-16		R.H. R.P.& D. as 6-4-16. 1 additional barn to Hannington for Road making 7 NCOs & men inoculated	
do	9-4-16		R.H. R.P.& D. as 6-4-16. Rifle Inspection. Received 1 Farrier from B # T D Campbell Lieut O.C. 3rd (av.) W Auxr H. T. Co.	

WAR DIARY
INTELLIGENCE SUMMARY
(Erase heading not required.)

Army Form C. 2118

Place	Date	Hour	Summary of Events and Information	Remarks and references to Appendices
FRUGES	10-4-16		Railhead MONTREUIL. Refilling point Supply Dump. Rue de STOMER FRUGES.	
do	11-4-16		Billets FRUGES R.H. R.P. & B. as 10-4-16 8 horses (L.D.) passed for casting by D.A.D.R. 1 Driver from D.R.S.	
do	12-4-16		R.H. R.P. & B. as 10-4-16 2/Lieut. Sendell returned from leave to U.K.	
do	13-4-16		R.H. R.P. & B. as 10-4-16 8 L.D. horses sent to 20th Mobile V Section Nos 54, 101,100, 31,132, 137, 108, 131 2 L.D. Horses received from Base via Railhead.	
do	14-4-16		R.H. R.P. & B. as 10-4-16 3 Drivers reported from B.H.T.D. present strength 1 surplus.	
do	15-4-16		R.H. R.P. & B. as 10-4-16 1 Driver from D.R.S. 1 Driver (from party attached to 1st Brigade) admitted to D.R.S.	A.P. Phelby Lieut O.C. 3rd Cav Div Ammn H.T. Coy.

WAR DIARY
INTELLIGENCE SUMMARY
(Erase heading not required.)

Place	Date	Hour	Summary of Events and Information	Remarks and references to Appendices
FRUGES	16-4-16		Railhead MONTREUIL. Refilling point Supply Dump Rue de STOMER FRUGES. Billets FRUGES. 1 Dr admitted to D.R.S.	
do	17-4-16		Inspected Men, horses etc attached to 7th Brigade at LA RAMONIERE FARM HUCQUELIERS. R.H. R.P.+B. as 16-4-16. 1 L.P. waggon with 1st L.G's. evacuated to O.O. Base 1 L.P. waggon sent to 1st L.G's to replace one evacuated. 6 G.S. waggons, 26 Horses, 13 Drivers, 1 Sergt. under 2 Lt Sendell sent to Cucq for Duty.	
do	18-4-16		R.H. R.P.+B. as 16-4-16. Inspected Billets.	
do	19-4-16		R.H. R.P.+B. as 16-4-16.	
do	20-4-16		R.H. R.P.+B. as 16-4-16. 1 Driver from D.R.S.	

C.P. Roller Lieut
O.C. 3rd Cav. Div. Aux H.T. Coy

Army Form C. 2118

WAR DIARY
or
INTELLIGENCE SUMMARY

(Erase heading not required.)

Instructions regarding War Diaries and Intelligence Summaries are contained in F. S. Regs., Part II. and the Staff Manual respectively. Title Pages will be prepared in manuscript.

Place	Date	Hour	Summary of Events and Information	Remarks and references to Appendices
FRUGES	21-4-16		Railhead MONTREUIL. Refilling Point. Supply Dump Rue de ST OMER FRUGES. Billets FRUGES.	
do	22-4-16		D/r Ridley appointed A/Lce Cpl from 6-4-16. 1 Driver ISS to DRS.	
do	23-4-16		R.H. RP tB co 21-4-16 R.A. RP tB co 21-4-16 Received 1 G.S. waggon from O.O Calais 3 LD horses (fillers) evacuated to No 20 M.V.S. 1 Driver + 1SS from DRS	
do	24-4-16		R.H RP tB co 21-4-16	
do	25-4-16		R.H RP tB co 21-4-16 1 man received from DRS	

CPModley Lieut
O.C. 3rd Cav. Div. Amac M.T. Coy

WAR DIARY
INTELLIGENCE SUMMARY
(Erase heading not required.)

Army Form C. 2118

Place	Date	Hour	Summary of Events and Information	Remarks and references to Appendices
FRUGES	26-4-16		Railhead MONTREUIL. Refilling Point Supply Dump Rue de STOMER FRUGES. Billets FRUGES Lieut. C.G.P. Kelly £ear to U.K. 27/4/16 to 4/5/16. 1 R Horse died	
do	27-4-16		R.H. R.P. ↑ 10. as 26-4-16. 8 L.D. Horses arrived from Base	
do	28-4-16		R.H. R.P. ↓ 3 as 26-4-16	
do	29-4-16		R.H. R.P. ↑ 3 as 26-4-16. 1 Driver from D.R.S.	
do	30-4-16		R.H. R.P. ↑ 3 as 26-4-16.	

C.G.P. Kelly Lieut.
O.C. 3rd Cav. Div. Aux. H.T. Coy.

Lof-   Annex H Tpt Coy   Army Form C. 2118
Vol 4

WAR DIARY
or
INTELLIGENCE SUMMARY
(Erase heading not required.)

Place	Date	Hour	Summary of Events and Information	Remarks and references to Appendices
FRUGES	1-5-16		Railhead BEAURAINVILLE. Refilling Point Supply Dump. Rue de ST OMER FRUGES. Billets FRUGES. 1 Driver sent on trial to H.Q. A.S.C. 1st Cav Div	
do	2-5-16		R.H. R.P. & B. as 1-5-16. 1 L.P. waggon to O.O Base (from Leicester Yeomanry) 1 L.P waggon sent to Leicester Yeomanry to replace one condemned. 1 Driver to D.R.S. Medical Inspection by D.A.D.M.S.	
do	3-5-16		R.H. R.P. & B. as 1-5-16. 1 Man to D.R.S.	
do	4-5-16		R.H. R.P. & B. as 1-5-16. 1 L.P waggon to O.O Base	
do	5-5-16		R.H. R.P. & B. as 1-5-16. 1 Man from D.R.S. 1 Driver received from H.Q. A.S.C. 1st Cav Div	

CJMellor Lieut.
OC. 3rd Cav Div Ammn. H.T.Co

Army Form C. 2118

WAR DIARY
or
INTELLIGENCE SUMMARY

(Erase heading not required.)

Instructions regarding War Diaries and Intelligence Summaries are contained in F. S. Regs., Part II. and the Staff Manual respectively. Title Pages will be prepared in manuscript.

Place	Date	Hour	Summary of Events and Information	Remarks and references to Appendices
FRUGES	6-5-16		Railhead BEAURAINVILLE Refilling Point Supply Dump Rue de St OMER. FRUGES. Billets FRUGES.	
do	7-5-16		R.H. R.P+B. as 6-5-16. 2 Drivers received from B.H.T.D	
do	8-5-16		R.H. R.P+B as 6-5-16. 2 G.S. waggons received from O.O Base. 1 Sgt reverted to A/Cpl.	
do	9-5-16		R.H. R.P+B as 6-5-16. 2 Riders + 2.L.D Horses received from Base.	
do	10-5-16		R.H. R.P+B as 6-5-16. Inspection of Horses by V.O. 1 Team waggon sent to BEAURAINVILLE for Remp Duty.	
do	11-5-16		R.H. R.P+B as 6-5-16. Lieut. C.G.R. WELLER returned from leave. C.G.R. Weller Lieut. O.C. 3rd Cav Div Amoc H.T.C.	

WAR DIARY
or
INTELLIGENCE SUMMARY
(Erase heading not required.)

Army Form C. 2118

Place	Date	Hour	Summary of Events and Information	Remarks and references to Appendices
FRUGES	12-5-16		Railhead BEAURAINVILLE. Refilling Point Supply Dump Rue de ST OMER FRUGES. Billets FRUGES.	
do	13-5-16		Inspection of Billets RW RPyB as 12-5-16. A/Cpl Graham appointed A/Sgt with pay from 6-5-16	
do	14-5-16		RW RPyB as 12-5-16. 1 L.D. Horse to M.V.S.	
do	15-5-16		RW RPyB as 12-5-16. 1 Driver to D.R.S.	
do	16-5-16		RW RPyB as 12-5-16.	
do	17-5-16		RW RPyB as 12-5-16. 3 L.P. waggons evacuated to O.O. Base 3 G.S. waggons received from O.O. Base	

GRodley Lieut
O.C. 3rd Cav. Div Amm. H.T. Co.

WAR DIARY
INTELLIGENCE SUMMARY
(Erase heading not required.)

Army Form C. 2118

Place	Date	Hour	Summary of Events and Information	Remarks and references to Appendices
FRUGES	18-5-16		Railhead BEAURAINVILLE. Refilling point Supply Dump Rue de STOMER FRUGES. Billets FRUGES.	
do	19-5-16		RH RP+B as 18-5-16	
do	20-5-16		RH RP+B as 18-5-16. Lieut C.G.R. Weller promoted Captain from 30-4-16.	
do	21-5-16		RH RP+B as 18-5-16	
do	22-5-16		RH RP +B as 18-5-16	
do	23-5-16		RH RP+B as 18-5-16	
do	24-5-16		RH. RP+B as 18-5-16. Capt Weller placed in charge of transport at HEZECQUES	
do	25-5-16		RH RP+B as 18-5-16. 2 trans. waggon H men sent to N.S.Y. Sgt Hughes to 5th reg't of Corps Pay. Graham do do Sterns do do Cpl. Sharpe to 7th reg't of Corps Pay.	

C.G.R. Weller, Capt.
O.C. 3rd Cav. Div. Aux. H.T. Co

WAR DIARY
or
INTELLIGENCE SUMMARY

(Erase heading not required.)

Army Form C. 2118

Place	Date	Hour	Summary of Events and Information	Remarks and references to Appendices
26-5-16 FRUGES	26-5-16		Railhead BEAURAINVILLE Refilling Point Supply Dump Rue de ST OMER FRUGES. Billets FRUGES	
	27-5-16		1 men "Shuck off" sent to Hospital by his regiment R.H R.P. 18 co 26-5-16 1 ham wagon returned from BEAURAINVILLE.	
	28-5-16		R.H RP-18 co 26-5-16	
	29-5-16		R.H RP-18 co 26-5-16. Horses picketed in field Rue Du MARAIS FRUGES.	
	30-5-16		R.H, R.P, + B. ao 26-5-16 Medical Inspection by A.D.M.S 2 L P wagons sent to D.O Base 2 G.S wagons received from D.O Base.	
	31-5-16		R.H RP+B co 26-5-16.	

CG Rosellen Capt.
O C 3rd Cav. Div. Ammn. H.T. Coy.

WAR DIARY
or
INTELLIGENCE SUMMARY

Army Form C. 2118

Place	Date	Hour	Summary of Events and Information	Remarks and references to Appendices
26-5-16 FRUGES	26-5-16		Railhead BEAURAINVILLE Refilling Point Supply Dump Rue de ST OMER FRUGES. Billets FRUGES. 1 man struck off, sent to Hospital by his regiment.	
	27-5-16		R.H. R.P.& B. on 26-5-16. 1 hav. wagon returned from BEAURAINVILLE.	
	28-5-16		R.H. R.P.& B. on 26-5-16.	
	29-5-16		R.H. R.P.& B. on 26-5-16. Horses picked up field Rue Du MARAIS, FRUGES.	
	30-5-16		R.H., R.P., & B. on 26-5-16. Medical Inspection by A.D.M.S. 2 L.P. wagons sent to D.O. Base. 2 Q.S. wagons received from D.O. Base.	
	31-5-16		R.H. R.P.& B. on 26-5-16.	

C.J. Miller. Capt.
O.C. 3rd Cav. Div. Aux. H.T. Coy.

3 Cav Div Aux H.T.Coy
A.C.C. 2 Echelon Jun
Vol I &

WAR DIARY
INTELLIGENCE SUMMARY
Army Form C. 2118

(Erase heading not required.)

Place	Date	Hour	Summary of Events and Information	Remarks and references to Appendices
FRUGES	1-6-16		Railhead BEAURAINVILLE Refilling Point Supply Dump Rue de St OMER FRUGES. Billets FRUGES.	
do	2-6-16		R.H. R.P. & B. as 1-6-16. 1 Cpl + 1 man to D.R.S.	
do	3-6-16		R.H. R.P.+B. as 1-6-16. Received 24 Tanks for fitting in G.S. waggons – no fittings received with them.	
do	4-6-16		R.H. R.P.+B. as 1-6-16.	
do	5-6-16		R.H. R.P.+B. as 1-6-16. Lieut. SEMDELL + 6 waggons now at VILLIERS	
do	6-6-16		R.H. R.P.+B. as 1-6-16. 1 man to D.R.S.	
do	6-6-16		R.H. R.P.+B. as 1-6-16. 2 Drs transferred to 4th Cav Fd Ambulance. 1 LD Horse from No 13 M.V.S.	
do	7-6-16.		Rd. R.P.+B as 1-6-16. 1 Ph. received from Essex Yeo.	

C.G. Robebler Capt.
O.C. 3rd Cav Div Aux H.T.Co

WAR DIARY or INTELLIGENCE SUMMARY

Army Form C. 2118

(Erase heading not required.)

Place	Date	Hour	Summary of Events and Information	Remarks and references to Appendices
FRUGES	10-6-16		Railhead BEAURAINVILLE. Refilling Point Supply dump Rue de St OMER. FRUGES. Billets FRUGES. Sgt. Sterno + 8 teams returned from roadmaking in 4th Bde.	
do	11-6-16		RH RP+B as 10-6-16	
do	12-6-16		RH RP+D as 10-6-16	
do	13-6-16		RH RP+D as 10-6-16. Capt C/Moller to Hospital.	
do	14-6-16		RH RP+B as 10-6-16. Time advanced by 1 hr at 11 pm.	
do	15-6-16		RH RP+B as 10-6-16	
do	16-6-16		RH RP+B as 10-6-16	
do	17-6-16		RH RP+B as 10-6-16. 4 LD stores to No 20 Mobile Vet Sec. 1 Driver to No 26 Gnl SP. 1 man from DRS.	

C/Moller Capt.
O.C. 3rd Cav Div Amm Sub.C.

WAR DIARY
INTELLIGENCE SUMMARY
(Erase heading not required.)

Army Form C. 2118

Instructions regarding War Diaries and Intelligence Summaries are contained in F. S. Regs., Part II. and the Staff Manual respectively. Title Pages will be prepared in manuscript.

Place	Date	Hour	Summary of Events and Information	Remarks and references to Appendices
FRUGES	18-6-16		Railhead BEAURAINVILLE Refilling Point Supply Dump Rue de ST OMER FRUGES. Billets FRUGES. 1 Cpl from D.R.S.	
do	19-6-16		R.H. R.P. & Bos 18-6-16	
do	20-6-16		R.H. R.P. & Bos 18-6-16 Received orders to call in waggons from Regiments and to proceed to ABBEVILLE on 21st to have waggons fitted with water tanks. Capt. C.G.R. Bottler returned from hospital.	
do	21-6-16		Company marched from FRUGES at 3. P.M. en route for ABBEVILLE arriving at LE BOISLE at 9 p.m.	
LE BOISLE	22-6-16		Company marched from LE BOISLE arriving at ABBEVILLE. Cpl Sharpe to Base Hospital, resulting to Divn in consequence. L/Cpl Bailey appointed full Cpl with Pay.	
ABBEVILLE	23-6-16		Refilling Point & Billets Advanced M.T. Depot ABBEVILLE. 17 L.P. + 1 G.S. waggon Mark IV changed for Mark X waggons. Received 7 G.S. waggons fitted with tanks from A.M.T.D.	Cy P Notter Capt. O.C. 3rd Cav. Div. Auxr. H.T.Co.

1875. Wt. W593/326 1,000,000 4/15 J.B.C. & A. A.D.S.S./Forms/C. 2118.

WAR DIARY
OF
INTELLIGENCE SUMMARY

(Erase heading not required.)

Army Form C. 2118

Place	Date	Hour	Summary of Events and Information	Remarks and references to Appendices
ABBEVILLE	24-6-16		Refilling Point & Billets A.H.T.D. ABBEVILLE. 1 Rider & 6 L.D. Horses evacuated to M.V.S ABBEVILLE 1 Rider & 11 L.D. Horses received from A.H.T.D 2 Farriers, 1 wheeler and 6 Drivers received from A.H.T.D	
ABBEVILLE	25-6-16		Received 30 mules from A.H.T.D to be attached. Received 15 R.F.A Drivers from A.H.T.D. 1 L.D. Horse to A.H.T.D (sick) Company marched from ABBEVILLE to ARGOEUVRES en route for CORBIE	
ARGOEUVRES	26-6-16		Company marched from ARGOEUVRES and reported to 13th Corps at CORBIE. Camped on Hill about 2 miles outside Town on BRAY road	
CORBIE	27-6-16		Dispatched 1 Sgt 1 Cpl 1 Sec Cpl 1 Farrier 22 Drivers 1 wheeler & 5 horses 10 waggons to 8th Corps at MARIEUX 1 Tpr to N° 38 CCS Mord from Camp on Hill to N° 13, a Camp in CORBIE	

G.M. Shellet Capt
O.C 3rd Cav. Div. Divnl. A.T.C

Army Form C. 2118

WAR DIARY
or
INTELLIGENCE SUMMARY
(Erase heading not required.)

Place	Date	Hour	Summary of Events and Information	Remarks and references to Appendices
CORBIE	28-6-16		Railhead HEILLY. Refilling Point 18th Corps Supply Dump CORBIE Camp Co CORBIE	Billets No B 2
			1 Officer 1 Sgt 1 Cpl 1 L/Cpl 2 Farriers 20 waggons 30 mules 51 horses 42 Drivers despatched to 30th Division at ETINEHAM	
CORBIE	29-6-16		R.H. R.P & B as 28-6-16	
do	30-6-16		R.H. R.P & B as 28-6-16	

CGPMallot Capt
O.C. 3rd Cav Div Aux. H.T.C.

WAR DIARY
or
INTELLIGENCE SUMMARY

Army Form C. 2118

3rd Cav Aux H.T. Coy

No 6

(Erase heading not required.)

Instructions regarding War Diaries and Intelligence Summaries are contained in F.S. Regs., Part II. and the Staff Manual respectively. Title Pages will be prepared in manuscript.

Place	Date	Hour	Summary of Events and Information	Remarks and references to Appendices
CORBIE	1-7-16		Railhead HEILLY Refilling Point 13th Corps Supply Dump CORBIE Billets Nº B2 Camp CORBIE.	
do	2-7-16		Dr McDougall R applt A/Sce Cpl with pay from 23-6-16. 1 L.D. Horse to M.V.S. 30th Div. 1 Pte joined from North Somerset Yeomanry.	
do	3-7-16		R.H. R.P. & B. as 1-7-16. 5 L.D Horses from Base Remounts.	
do	4-7-16		R.H. R.P. & B. as 1-7-16.	
do	5-7-16		R.H. R.P. & B. as 1-7-16.	
do	6-7-16		R.H. R.P. & B. as 1-7-16. Detacht. under Lieut SENDELL moved to 9th Div. 6 Cylindrical tanks changed for rectangular tanks at 6 R.E. Park MERICOURT.	
do	7-7-16		R.H. R.P. & B. as 1-7-16. 8 cyldl. tanks changed for rect tanks ditto.	
do	8-7-16		R.H. R.P. & B. as 1-7-16. 8 tanks changed as above.	

C.G. Plotter. Capt.
O.C. 3rd Cav. Div. Aux H.T.C.
attached XIII Corps.

WAR DIARY
INTELLIGENCE SUMMARY

Army Form C. 2118

Place	Date	Hour	Summary of Events and Information	Remarks and references to Appendices
CORBIE	9-7-16		Railhead HEILLY. Refilling Point 13th Corps Supply Dump CORBIE. Billets N° 132 Camp CORBIE. Pte. Linch (Filthy) joined from B.M.T.D. 8 cylindrical tanks changed for rectangular tanks at N°6 R.E. Park MERICOURT.	
do	10-7-16		R.H. R.P. & B. as 9-7-16. 8 tanks changed as above. H.Q. of Co moved from CORBIE to Bois de TAILLE (south) camp on road from CHIPILLY to ETINEHAM. 3.1 D horses to N° 40 M.V.S.	
Bois de TAILLE (South)	11-7-16		Railhead HEILLY. Refilling Point 13th Corps H.Q. Supply Dump CHIPILLY. Billets Bois de TAILLE (South).	
do	12-7-16		R.H. R.P. & B. as 11-7-16. 1 D^r. joined from B.M.T.D	
do	13-7-16		R.H. R.P. & B. as 11-7-16. 20 waggons horses & personel transferred from 30th Div to 3rd Div.	
do	14-7-16		R.H. R.P. & B. as 11-7-16. S.C.pl Storie A.R.A.M.C. returned to N° 12 San. Sec.	

O.C. 3rd Cav Div Aux H.T Co
attached XIII Corps.

C.G. Rholler. Capt.
O.C. 3rd Cav Div Aux H.T Co
attached XIII Corps.

Army Form C. 2118

WAR DIARY
or
INTELLIGENCE SUMMARY
(Erase heading not required.)

Instructions regarding War Diaries and Intelligence Summaries are contained in F.S. Regs., Part II. and the Staff Manual respectively. Title Pages will be prepared in manuscript.

Place	Date	Hour	Summary of Events and Information	Remarks and references to Appendices
Bois du TAILLÉ (South)	15.7.16		Railhead NEILLY. Refilling point 13th Corps Ad Qrs dump (M) PILLY Billets Bois de TAILLE (South)	
do	16.7.16		1 L.D horse to M.V.S	
do	17.7.16		R.H. R.P.+B. as 15-7-16.	
do	18.7.16		R.H. R.P.+B. as 15-7-16. Inspection of Co's Hd Qr horses by V.O.	
			R.H. R.P.+B. as 15.7.16	
do	19.7.16		R.H. R.P.+B. as 15.7.16.	
do	20.7.16		R.H. R.P.+B. as 15.7.16.	
do	21.7.16		R.H. R.P.+B. as 15.7.16. 10 waggons/H.Horses + 23 men sent to 30th Div to be temporarily attached.	
do	22.7.16		R.d R.P.+B. as 15.7.16	
do	23.7.16		Rd. R.P.+B. as 15.7.16.	

C.P. Rotter Capt.
O.C. 3rd Cav. Div. Amm. Sd. T.C.
Attached XIII Corps.

Army Form C. 2118

WAR DIARY
or
INTELLIGENCE SUMMARY
(Erase heading not required.)

Instructions regarding War Diaries and Intelligence Summaries are contained in F. S. Regs., Part II. and the Staff Manual respectively. Title Pages will be prepared in manuscript.

Place	Date	Hour	Summary of Events and Information	Remarks and references to Appendices
Bois de TAILLE (South)	24.7.16		Railhead HEILLY Refilling point 18th Corps Hd Qrs Dump CHIPILLY Billets Bois de TAILLE (South)	
do	25.9.16		R.H. R.P. + B as 24.7.16. S.S.M. Lyons to Hospital.	
do	26.7.16		R.H. R.P. + B as 24.7.16. Hd Qr Camp moved to ETINEHEM	
do	27.7.16		R.H. R.P. + B as 24.7.16. 10 Tour wagons, Horses + Personnel transferred from 3rd Div to 55th Div Train 3rd Div to 2nd Div	
do	28.7.16		R.H. R.P. + B as 24.7.16.	
do	29.7.16		R.H. R.P. + B as 24.7.16. S.S.M Lyons returned from Hospital to Hd Qrs Company	
do	30.7.16		R.H. R.P. + B as 24.7.16.	
do	31.7.16		R.H. R.P. + B as 24.7.16. I visited each detachment every other day, and frequently accompanied the wagons at their work.	

C.G. Wollen Capt.
O.C. 3rd Cav Div. H.T. Co. Attached XIII Corps.

WAR DIARY
or
INTELLIGENCE SUMMARY
(Erase heading not required.)

Army Form C. 2118

3 Cav H T Coy

Vol 7

Place	Date	Hour	Summary of Events and Information	Remarks and references to Appendices
N- ETINEHEM	1-8-16		Railhead HEILLY Refilling Point MORLANCOURT. Billets Camp near ETINEHEM. 1 Driver to Hospital.	
do	2-8-16		R'd R&B as 1-8-16 5 Tank wagons, 25 Horses + personnel returned from 3ᵈ Div. to 6. Qd Qrs. 1 — 4 — 4 S Lancs 2 — 8 — 55ᵗʰ D.A.C. 2 — 8 — 55ᵗʰ Div Field Amb. 2 Drivers	
do	3-8-16		R'd R&B as 1-8-16. 4 damaged Tanks changed A Cpl Bownes & received 10 Drivers.	
do	4-8-16		R'd R&B as 1-8-16. 4 damaged Tanks changed.	
do	5-8-16		R'd R&B as 1-8-16. Pte Irwin B & Pte Packer W.J. of 1ˢᵗ L.G.'s severely wounded by shellfire. 4 horses L.D. killed. 1 Tank wagon damaged	

C Q M Sgt Mallon Capt.
O C 3ʳᵈ Cav D. n Amm H T Co

WAR DIARY
or
INTELLIGENCE SUMMARY

(Erase heading not required.)

Army Form C. 2118

Instructions regarding War Diaries and Intelligence Summaries are contained in F.S. Regs., Part II. and the Staff Manual respectively. Title Pages will be prepared in manuscript.

Place	Date	Hour	Summary of Events and Information	Remarks and references to Appendices
M ÉTINEHEM	6-8-16		Railhead HEILLY Refilling Point MORLANCOURT. Billets Camp M ÉTINEHEM. 1 tank damaged by shell fire sent in from 2nd Div. 1 L.D Horse killed by shell fire.	
do	4.8.16		R.H RP&B as 6-8-16. 1 damaged tank changed	
do	6.8.16		R.H RP&B as 6.8.16. 1 extra tank wagon sent to Detch with 2nd Div	
do	9.8.16		R.H RP&B as 6.8.16 Received from Remounts 1 Rider 7 mules	
do	10.8.16		R.H. RP&B as 6.8.16 10 wagons 45 horses & personnel returned from 2nd Div.	
do	11.8.16		R.H. RP&B as 6.8.16. S.t. Sendell, 4 tank wagons Horses + Personnel formed camp at MINDEN POST advanced	

C.J. Rholler Capt.
O.C. 3rd Cav Div Divi H.T.Co

WAR DIARY
or
INTELLIGENCE SUMMARY
(Erase heading not required.)

Army Form C. 2118

Place	Date	Hour	Summary of Events and Information	Remarks and references to Appendices
Mt ETINEHEM	12.8.16		Railhead HEILLY. Refilling Point MORLANCOURT. Billets Mt ETINEHEM MINDEN POST. 1 L.D. Horse killed by shell fire. 1 Tank wagon, 2 drivers, 4 horses attached to advanced camp MINDEN POST. A Cpl Park horse arrived from B.H.T.D.	
do	13-8-16		R.H. R.P & B as 12.8.16. Cpl Smith & 2 tank wagons sent to Minden Post.	
do	14.8.16		R.H. R.P & B as 12.8.16.	
do	15.8.16		R.H. R.P & B as 12.8.16. Cpl Bailey + 15 Tank wagons from 55th Div	
do	16.8.16		R.H. R.P & B as 12.8.16. Reserve camp formed at Great Bear Wood. 15 Tank wagons, horses and personnel under S.S.t Lyons. Pte Finch (MT Fitter) to Hospital.	

C.G. Walker Capt.
O.C. 3rd Cav Div Amm H T Co

Army Form C. 2118

WAR DIARY
or
INTELLIGENCE SUMMARY
(Erase heading not required.)

Instructions regarding War Diaries and Intelligence Summaries are contained in F. S. Regs., Part II. and the Staff Manual respectively. Title Pages will be prepared in manuscript.

Place	Date	Hour	Summary of Events and Information	Remarks and references to Appendices
Nr ETINEHEM	17.8.16		Railhead HEILLY Refilling Point MORLANCOURT Billets Camp Nr ETINEHEM MINDEN POST GREAT BEAR WOOD	
			1 tank wagon destroyed by shell fire.	
do	16.8.16		R.H. R.P. & B as 17.8.16.	Week ending 18th inst.
			Sent 2 tank wagons Complete to advance camp	7400 gals water
			1 Driver to Hospital.	returned to BERNAFY WOOD
			Advanced camp moved from MINDEN POST to F.17 c.o.3	500 gals to BRIQUETERIE
do	19.8.16		R.H. R.P. & B as 17.8.16	
			1 Driver to Hospital	
do	20.8.16		R.H. R.P. & B as 17.8.16.	
			1 Driver to Hospital	
do	21.8.16		R.H. R.P. & B as 17.8.16	
			Adv Gp. of Co. moved from ETINEHEM to MEAULTE	

C P Weller Capt.
O.C. 3rd Cav. Div Amn STC

WAR DIARY
or
INTELLIGENCE SUMMARY

(Erase heading not required.)

Army Form C. 2118

Instructions regarding War Diaries and Intelligence Summaries are contained in F. S. Regs., Part II. and the Staff Manual respectively. Title Pages will be prepared in manuscript.

Place	Date	Hour	Summary of Events and Information	Remarks and references to Appendices
MEAULTE	22.8.16		Railhead HEILLY Refilling point MORLANCOURT Billets Mr MEAULTE F17 C 03 GREAT BEAR WOOD	
do	23.8.16		R.H. R.P & B. as 22.8.16. 1 Mule to advanced camp 1 Horse changed with advanced camp	
do	24.8.16		R.H. R.P & B. as 22.8.16.	
do	25.8.16		R.H. R.P & B. as 22.8.16. 2 Drivers 1 team changed with advanced camp. Week ending 25th inst. 13,000 gals delivered at BERNAFY WOOD) BRIQUETERIE 1200 ——— to regiments Various ——— to regiments reating	
do	26.8.16		R.H. R.P & B. as 22.8.16. 1 Driver to Hospital (Enteric fever) 3 teams mules, wagons & personnel from S.S.M. Lyons debited to St Sendells advanced camp.	

C.G.Pheller Capt.
O.C. 3rd Cav Div Amm A.T.C

WAR DIARY
INTELLIGENCE SUMMARY
(Erase heading not required.)

Army Form C. 2118

Place	Date	Hour	Summary of Events and Information	Remarks and references to Appendices
Nr MEAULTE	27.8.16		Railhead HEILLY. Refilling Point MORLANCOURT Billets Camp Nr MEAULTE F17 C 03 GREAT BEARWOOD	
			Lce Cpl Kirby deprived of Lance stripe	
			1 Driver + pair exchanged with advanced camp.	
			3 Drivers from B.H.T.D	
do	28.8.16		RH RP+ D ao 27.8.16	
			1 Driver from B.H.T.D.	
			1 Driver to SS Madyans	
do	29.8.16		RH RP+B ao 27.8.16	
			SSM Lyons appointed Act'g SSM	
do	30.8.16		RH RP+B ao 27.8.16.	
			1 Driver to Hospital.	
			1 wagon exchanged with advanced camp.	
do	31.8.16		RH RP+D ao 27.8.16.	
			2 Drivers returned from Hospital	

C V Boller Capt.
D.C. 3rd Cav Div Amm H T C

WAR DIARY or INTELLIGENCE SUMMARY

Army Form C. 2118

Aus 1.? Coy

Vol 8

(Erase heading not required.)

Instructions regarding War Diaries and Intelligence Summaries are contained in F. S. Regs., Part II. and the Staff Manual respectively. Title Pages will be prepared in manuscript.

Place	Date	Hour	Summary of Events and Information	Remarks and references to Appendices
Mr MEAULTE	1-9-16		Railhead HEILLY. Refilling Point Supply Dump MORLANCOURT. Billets Camp Mr MEAULTE.	
			1 Driver to Hospital	week ending 1st Sept.
			1 Wagon & Tank changed for advanced Camp.	12,000 Gallons water to BERNAFAY Wood
			2 G.S. Wagons received from O.O. Base	3000 BRIQUETTERIE
				also Water to Requisite Resting
do	2-9-16		R.H R.P & B as 1-9-16	
			Received from A.H.T.D 2 Drivers & 1 D. Horses 1 G.S Wagon	
do	3-9-16		R.H R.P & B as 1-9-16.	
			1 Trooper to Hospital	
			1 D. Horse Changed for Advanced Camp.	
			1 Driver sent to Advanced Camp	
do	4-9-16		R.H R.P & B as 1-9-16	
			1 D. Horse evacuated to No 32 M.V.S.	
			3 New rectangular Tanks received from No 6 advanced R E Park	
do	5-9-16		R.H R.P & B as 1-9-16	
			a/Cpl Smith to Hospital	
			20 Horses, 3 Pumps received from No 6 advanced R E Park	

C.G.R. Kelly Capt.
O/C 3rd Cav. Div. Auxi. H.T. Co.

WAR DIARY

INTELLIGENCE SUMMARY

(Erase heading not required.)

Army Form C. 2118

Place	Date	Hour	Summary of Events and Information	Remarks and references to Appendices
Mt MEAULTE	3-9-16		Railhead HEILLY Refilling Point Supply Dump MORLANCOURT Billets Camp Mt MEAULTE. 1 Driver received from Hospital	
do	4-9-16		R.H. R.P. + B. as 3-9-16. 1 Tank wagon changed for advanced camp — undercarriage having been blown to pieces by shell fire. 1 Body of G.S. wagon received from	
do	5-9-16		R.H. R.P. + B. as 3-9-16 week ending 5th Sept. 11,200 gals water delivered to BERNAFAY WOOD 3,000 " " " " BRIQUETTERIE also water to Regiments resting.	
do	6-9-16		R.H. R.P. + B. as 3-9-16. 5 L.D. Horses received from Remounts to replace mules. 1 L.D. Horse sent to Guards Divn M.V.S. (Shrapnel wounds)	
do	10-9-16		R.H. R.P. + B. as 3-9-16. 2 Tank wagons changed for advanced camp. 1 Team changed for 1 Mule sent to	

C.G.Robbin. Capt.
O.C. 3rd Cav. Divn. Aux. H.T.C.

WAR DIARY
OF
INTELLIGENCE SUMMARY
(Erase heading not required.)

Army Form C. 2118

Place	Date	Hour	Summary of Events and Information	Remarks and references to Appendices
Mr MEALTE	11-9-16		Railhead HEILLY. Refilling Point Supply Dump MORLANCOURT. Billets Camp Mr MEALTE. 30 wagons, horses + personnel from 20th Res Park arrived to relieve Coy J water duties.	
do	12-9-16		RH R.P.PS as 11-9-16. Handed over 30 Tank Wagons pump hoses etc to officer i/c detachment 20th Res Pk. Received 30 G/S Wagons from — Handed over 5 surplus mules to No 6 Divnl Train	
do	13-9-16		RH & R.P as 11-9-16. Co moved from 14th Corps Mr MEALTE & rejoined 3rd Cav Div DAOURS. 5 days ending 13th Sept. 11,000 gals water delivered to BERNAFAY WOOD 2000 BRIQUETTERIE also water to Regiments resting.	
do	14-9-16 DAOURS			

C.P. Weller. Capt.
OC 3rd Cav Div Amm SS. T.Co

WAR DIARY
or
INTELLIGENCE SUMMARY

(Erase heading not required.)

Army Form C. 2118

Place	Date	Hour	Summary of Events and Information	Remarks and references to Appendices
DAOURS	14-9-16		Railhead FRÉCHENCOURT. Refilling Point CORBIE. Billets Camp DAOURS. No 3 Section rejoined Company from 46th Res Park. Wagons loaded up with Ammunition received from 3rd Cav Div Amm Park. 1350 rounds of High Explosive 1350 — Shrapnel 534,000 — Small Arms Ammunition 1800 — Hand Grenades ——— Gun parts, spare gun wheels etc. Sergt Long R.H.A. temporarily attached to Company from 3rd C.D. Amm Park. Lce Cpl McLean appointed A/Cpl with pay from 6-9-16 Dr Collins G a/Lcpl 6-9-16 Dr King H a/Lcpl 27-8-16 Dr Gilholm W a/Lcpl without pay	
Do	15-9-16		R.H. R.P. 13 as 14-9-16. Changed Camp to spot adjoining DAOURS Railhead. Sad/Cpl Finch returned to Dr Sadr.	

C.J. Rottley. Cpl
3rd Car Div Amm & T.C.

O.C. 3rd Car Div Amm & T.C.

WAR DIARY
or
INTELLIGENCE SUMMARY

(Erase heading not required.)

Army Form C. 2118

Place	Date	Hour	Summary of Events and Information	Remarks and references to Appendices
DAOURS	16-9-16		Railhead FRECHENCOURT. Refilling point CORBIE. Billets Camp DAOURS. 1 Driver to Hospital. 1 G.S. wagon received from O.O Base	
do	17-9-16		R.H R.P & B. as 16-9-16.	
do	18-9-16		R.H & B. as 16-9-16 Refilling Point 3rd Cav Div Supply Dump DAOURS. 4 R.F.A drivers admitted to Hospital. Sgt. Haines A.V.C joined from No 2 Vet Hospital	
do	19-9-16		R.H. R.P & B. as 18-9-16. 1 Driver Evacuated sick	
do	20-9-16		R.H R.P & B. as 18-9-16. 1 Driver joined from B. H T.D 3 Drivers to No 6 C. F.A.	
do	21-9-16		R.H. R.P & B. as 18-9-16. Pte Bailey ASC MT sent to B.M T.D 1 Driver to No 6 C.F.A 2 Drivers evacuated to No 20 M.V.S	C.P.Walker Capt. O.C. 3rd Cav Div Auck T Co.

1875. W. W. W 593/826 1,000,000 4/15 J.B.C. & A. A.D.S.S./Forms/C. 2118.

WAR DIARY
or
INTELLIGENCE SUMMARY
(Erase heading not required.)

Army Form C. 2118

Place	Date	Hour	Summary of Events and Information	Remarks and references to Appendices
DAOURS	22-9-16		Railhead FRÉCHENCOURT. Refilling point 3rd (?) Supply Dump DAOURS. Billets Camp DAOURS. Sergt Long R.A returned to 3rd Cav Div Amm. Park. Gun parts Gun wheels etc returned to Company evacuated to Secunderabad M.V.S. 1 Rider evacuated to Secunderabad M.V.S.	
do	23-9-16		R.H. R.P.'s as 22-9-16. Sgt Cuming R.T.A joined from 3rd Cav Div Amm. Park.	
do	24-9-16		R.H. R.P. as 22-9-16. Refilling Point CORBIE. 1 R.T.A. driver discharged from Hospital. 1 Rider received from Remounts 4th Army.	
do	25-9-16		R.H. R.P. as 24-9-16. 1st Anniversary of formation of Company.	
do	26-9-16		R.H. R.P. as 24-9-16.	

C.R.Miller. Capt
O.C 3rd Cav Div Amm H.T Co

WAR DIARY
or
INTELLIGENCE SUMMARY

Army Form C. 2118

Place	Date	Hour	Summary of Events and Information	Remarks and references to Appendices
DAOURS	27-9-16		Railhead FRECHENCOURT. Refilling Point CORBIE Billets Camp DAOURS. All ammunition carried on wagons dumped at ammunition Railhead CONTAY. S.S.M Lyons 4Tracuard rich to Lucknow C.C.S	
do	28-9-16		R.H & C. as 27-9-16. Refilling Point FRECHENCOURT. Company shapecled 2 R.F.A Drivers to Lucknow C.C.S by D.St.T.Cav Corps 2 L.D Horses received from Remounts.	
do	29-9-16		R.H. R.P+B as 28-9-16.	
do	30-9-16		R.H. R.P+D as 28-9-16 , R.F.A Driver discharged from Lucknow C.C.S	

A.J.Chottler. Capt
O.C. 3rd Cav Div Divor A.T.Co

… **WAR DIARY** or **INTELLIGENCE SUMMARY**

Army Form C. 2118

Place	Date	Hour	Summary of Events and Information	Remarks and references to Appendices
DAOURS	1-10-16		Railhead and Refilling Point FRECHENCOURT. Billets Camp DAOURS.	

Army Form C. 2118

WAR DIARY
INTELLIGENCE SUMMARY
(Erase heading not required.)

Place	Date	Hour	Summary of Events and Information	Remarks and references to Appendices
DAOURS	1-10-16		Railhead and Refilling Point FRECHENCOURT. Billets Camp N° DAOURS.	
			1 Driver to Base H.P.	
do	2-10-16		R.H. RP+B a 1-10-16.	
			D' Walker C Special leave to U.K.	
do	3-10-16		R.H. RP+B a 1-10-16	
			1 Driver to H.P.	
do	4-10-16		R.H. RP+B a 1-10-16	
			1 Rider 9 LD. to No4 M.V.S. CORBIE. 3 Drivers to H.P. 2 Drivers received from B.H.T.D.	
do	5-10-16		R.H. RP+B a 1-10-16.	
			2 Drivers to H.P.	
			1 — received from H.P.	
do	6-10-16		R.H. RP+B a 1-10-16	
do	7-10-16		R.H. RP+B a 1-10-16.	
			2 L.D. horses from Base remounts. 1 Driver from H.P.	
do	8-10-16		R.H. RP+B a 1-10-16.	
			D' Barnett Special leave to U.K. 1 Driver from H.P. 2 Drivers 2 H.P.	
			2 Horses Evacuated to No 15 M.V.S.	

C.P.Welch Capt.
O.C. 3rd Cav. Div. Aux. H.T.Co

WAR DIARY or INTELLIGENCE SUMMARY

Army Form C. 2118

(Erase heading not required.)

Place	Date	Hour	Summary of Events and Information	Remarks and references to Appendices
DAOURS.	9-10-16		Railhead and Refilling Point FRECHENCOURT Billets Camp Nº DAOURS 40 wagons loaded with 5½ tons oats received from Supply Column 3rd Cav Div (6 wks short) 1 Driver to SP.	
do	10-10-16		RH RP+B co 9-10-16. 1 Driver from SP.	
do	11-10-16		RH. RP+B co 9-10-16 1 Driver from SP.	
do	12-10-16		RH. RP+B co 9-10-16	
do	13-10-16		RH RP+B co 9-10-16 1 Driver from SP Inspection of Company by D.S+T & 2nd army	
do	14-10-16		RH. RP+B co 9-10-16 1 LD Horse to No 35 M.V.S.	
do	15-10-16		RH. RP+B co 9-10-16. 6 Drivers from B.H.T.D.	
do	16-10-16		RH. RP+Bco 9-10-16. Special leave for Dr Walker extended to 14th Inst.	
do	17-10-16		RH. RP+B co 9-10-16. 2 unserviceable bicycles returned to Base.	
do	18-10-16		RH. RP+B co 9-10-16.	
do	19-10-16		RH. RP+B co 9-10-16. 1 Dr to SP	
do	20-10-16		RH. RP+B co 9-10-16. 1 LD Horse destroyed.	

A.P.Moeller Capt.
O.C. 3rd Cav Div Divl H.T.C.

WAR DIARY
or
INTELLIGENCE SUMMARY

Army Form C. 2118

Place	Date	Hour	Summary of Events and Information	Remarks and references to Appendices
DAOURS.	21-10-16		Railhead and Refilling Point. FRECHENCOURT. Billets Camp Nr DAOURS. 2 Drivers to AP. 4 Drivers received from B.H.T.D.	
do	22-10-16		RH. RP. + B. Co. 21-10-16. Dumped 8 tons of oats for 3 R.H.A. Batteries on AMIENS–DOULLENS Road 2 Drivers from AP. Took own lorry to shed for Farriers shop.	
do	23-10-16		RH. RP. + B. Co. 21-10-16. 1 Driver to AP.	
do	24-10-16		RH. RP. + B. Co. 21-10-16.	
do	25-10-16		RH. RP. + B. Co. 21-10-16.	
do	26-10-16		RH. RP. + B. Co. 21-10-16. 2L.D. + 2 Riders received from Base Remounts. 1 Dr. to AP	
do	27-10-16		RH. RP. + B. Co. 21-10-16.	
do	28-10-16		RH. RP. + B. Co. 21-10-16. 1 Dr. from AP. 1 Dr. to AP.	
do	29-10-16		RH. RP. + B. Co. 21-10-16.	
do	30-10-16		RH. RP. + B. Co. 21-10-16. Took over Farriers shop in DAOURS.	
do	31-10-16		RH. RP. + B. Co. 21-10-16. Gave up lean-to Farriers shop near Camp.	

C.P. Wheller Capt.
O.C. 3rd Cav. Div. Aux. H.T. Co

WAR DIARY
or
INTELLIGENCE SUMMARY.
(Erase heading not required.)

Army Form C. 2118.

Place	Date	Hour	Summary of Events and Information	Remarks and references to Appendices
DAOURS	1-11-16		Railhead & Refilling Point FRECHENCOURT. Billets Camp Nº DAOURS. 1 Drvr to Hospital	
do	2-11-16		RH. RP+B as 1-11-16. Dumped 46 tons of oats at the Barques CORBIE.	
			1 Drvr to Hospital. 3 Drvrs from Hospital.	
do	3-11-16		Company marched from VECQUEMONT to VIGNACOURT	
do	4-11-16		Company marched from VIGNACOURT to BRAILLY	
do	5-11-16		Company marched from BRAILLY to BEAURAINVILLE	
BEAURAINVILLE	6-11-16		Railhead, Refilling Point & Billets BEAURAINVILLE	
			1 Drvr to Hospital	
do	7-11-16		RH. RP+B as 6-11-16. A/Cpl McLean returned to Duty.	
do	8-11-16		RH. RP+B as 6-11-16.	
do	9-11-16		RH. RP+B as 6-11-16. 6 wagons + teams complete issued to 6th Bde. 2 to each Regt	
			6 " 4th Bde at AVONDANCE	
			1 NCO. 8 " Cavalry Corps at REGNIERE ECLUSE.	
			Pte Graham H. Essex Yeomanry, rejoined from Regt.	
do	10-11-16		RH. RP+B as 6-11-16	
			2 teams each carrying Rations from Railhead to 3 Regts.	

McNeill Cpl.
O.C. 3rd Cav. Div. Amm. M.T.C.

WAR DIARY or INTELLIGENCE SUMMARY

Army Form C. 2118.

Place	Date	Hour	Summary of Events and Information	Remarks and references to Appendices
BEAURAINVILLE	11-11-16		Railhead, Refilling Point & Billets BEAURAINVILLE Started Carrying Rations for R+G	
do	12-11-16		RH RP+B as 11-11-16.	
do	13-11-16		RH RP+B as 11-11-16.	
do	14-11-16		RH RP+B as 11-11-16.	
do	15-11-16		RH RP+B as 11-11-16. Capt. McMullen legue to England from 15-11-16 to 24-11-16	
do	16-11-16		RH RP+B as 11-11-16. Lt G. John to leave to England from 16-11-16 to 25-11-16.	
do	17-11-16		S.S.M. Joll C. reported for Duty from 37th Div Train.	
do	18-11-16		RH RP+B as 11-11-16. 3 wagons drawn to Leicester Yrs for Duty.	
do	19-11-16		RH RP+B as 11-11-16. 1 R.F.A. Driver from Hospital.	
do	20-11-16		RH RP+B as 11-11-16.	
do	21-11-16		RH RP+B as 11-11-16. 3 Surplus Drivers returned to Base (H.T+S)	
do	22-11-16		RH RP+B as 11-11-16.	
do	23-11-16		RH RP+B as 11-11-16.	
do	24-11-16		RH RP+B as 11-11-16.	

McMullen Capt.
OC No 3 Cav. Div. Amm H.T. Co

Army Form C. 2118.

WAR DIARY
or
INTELLIGENCE SUMMARY.
(Erase heading not required.)

Instructions regarding War Diaries and Intelligence Summaries are contained in F. S. Regs., Part II. and the Staff Manual respectively. Title pages will be prepared in manuscript.

Place	Date	Hour	Summary of Events and Information	Remarks and references to Appendices
BEAURAINVILLE	25-11-16		Railhead MARESQUEL. Billets BEAURAINVILLE. Company moved to ST DENOEUX. 2 L.D. Horses + 2 Mules from Base Remounts.	
ST DENOEUX	26-11-16		Railhead MARESQUEL. Refilling Point MARESQUEL. Billets ST DENOEUX.	
do	27-11-16		R# RP+D as 26-11-16	
do	28-11-16		RS RP+D as 26-11-16	
			6 wagons trains to B.T.O. 8th Bde BEAURAINVILLE	
			3 " " " 1st Life Guards FRESSIN	
			2 " " " 2nd M.G. Sqdn CREQUEY	
			1 " " " 1st Essex Yeo. AUBIN ST YAAST	
			2 " " " R.H. Gds AIX EN ISSANT	
			2 " " " 10th Hussars MARESQUEL	
do	29-11-16		R# RP+D as 26-11-16. 1 Dvr. to Hospital	
			1 Officer, 1 WO, 90 R+F (3 Four, 3 saddle, 2 wheelers) 118 L.D Horses 5 Riders	
			14 Mules 30 wagons attached from 3rd Cav Div Rec Pk	
do	30-11-16		R# RP+D as 26-11-16	
			Sgt. ASNINE. Glo. returned to 3rd C. Amm. Park	
			Cpl. Packhouse sent to BTO 8th Cav Bde in charge of wagons.	

O.C. 3rd Cav Div. Rec Pk.

[Signature] Capt.
O.C. 3rd Cav Div. Aug 1/16

WAR DIARY
or
INTELLIGENCE SUMMARY.
(Erase heading not required.)

Army Form C. 2118.

Place	Date	Hour	Summary of Events and Information	Remarks and references to Appendices
ST DENOEUX	1-12-16		Railhead MARESQUEL Refilling Point MARESQUEL Billets ST DENOEUX 2 Lieut. C H Sendall went on leave to U.K. 2nd to 12th. 1 man returned from R & G's	
do	2-12-16		R & RP + 13 OR 1-12-16	
do	3-12-16		R & RP + B OR 1-12-16	
do	4-12-16		R H RP + B OR 1-12-16. 1 Cpl 6 horses to 6th Cav Bde. } of 5th Cav Res Pk 1 Sergt 6 horses to 7th Cav BDE } to rel 50 horses	
do	5-12-16		1 WO 5th Cav Res Pk returned to Hosp 5th Cav Res Pk. RH RP + B OR 1-12-16. 4 Drivers 5th Cav Res Pk to Hospital 1 Driver Anc H T Co do	
do	6-12-16		R H RP + B OR 1-12-16	
do	7-12-16		R H RP + 10 OR 1-12-16 1 team to 6th Cav Bde } From 5th Cav Res Pk. 6 men 1 — 7th — } 2 horses 1 — 8th — 1 L D of 5th Cav Res Pk Evacuated to M.V.S.	

C G Rochlin Capt.
O.C. 3rd Cav Div Anur H T Co

Army Form C. 2118.

WAR DIARY
or
INTELLIGENCE SUMMARY.
(Erase heading not required.)

Instructions regarding War Diaries and Intelligence Summaries are contained in F.S. Regs., Part II. and the Staff Manual respectively. Title pages will be prepared in manuscript.

Place	Date	Hour	Summary of Events and Information	Remarks and references to Appendices
ST DENOEUX	7-12-16 (contd)		Railhead + Refilling Point MARESQUEL Billets ST DENOEUX	
			1 Driver to Hospital	
do	8-12-16		R.H. R.P.+B. as 7-12-16. 1 team mules to 7th Bde.	
do	9-12-16		R.H. R.P.+B. as 7-12-16. 1 Sgt. Gn. 1 Driver 2 Riders 1 team horses to 7th Bde. 1 team horses & 1 team mules to 7th Bde. A.V.C.	
			40 I.D. 8 mules, 12 wagons 30 O.R. 5th Cav. Bde R.P. to CAMPIGNEULLES LES PETITES.	
do	10-12-16		R.H. R.P.+B. as 7-12-16. 1 Driver from Hospital	
do	11-12-16		R.H. R.P.+B. as 7-12-16. 1 Driver 5th Cav Bde R.P. from Hospital.	
			Capt Kotler inspected Transport with Cav Corps	
do	12-12-16		R.H. R.P.+B. as 7-12-16	
do	13-12-16		R.H. R.P.+B. as 7-12-16. 2 Drivers 1 team to R.H.Q's 1 Sgt to Cav Corps to be in charge of Transport	
do	14-12-16		R.H. R.P.+B. as 7-12-16. 1 Driver to Hospital	
			Capt Kotler inspected transport with 7th Cav Bde.	
do	15-12-16		R.H. R.P.+B. as 7-12-16. 1 Driver to Div Rest Station	

CPRotler Capt.
O.C. 3rd Cav. Div. Auxx H.T.C.

Army Form C. 2118.

WAR DIARY
or
INTELLIGENCE SUMMARY.
(Erase heading not required.)

Instructions regarding War Diaries and Intelligence Summaries are contained in F. S. Regs., Part II. and the Staff Manual respectively. Title pages will be prepared in manuscript.

Place	Date	Hour	Summary of Events and Information	Remarks and references to Appendices
ST DENOEUX	16-12-16		Railhead & Refilling Point MARESQUEL Billets ST DENOEUX. 3 Drivers from HQ 5th Cav Res Pk for Det. 5 Cav Pk	
do	17-12-16		RH RP&B as 16-12-16	
do	18-12-16		RH RP&B as 16-12-16 Capt Letellier inspected Transport with 6th Cav Bde. Cooking Parade.	
do	19-12-16		RH RP&B as 16-12-16	
do	20-12-16		RH RP&B as 16-12-16 1LD Horse No 197 to No 20 MVS.	
do	21-12-16		1LD Horse from 10th Hussars HQ of Coy moved from St Denoeux to BEAURAINVILLE	
BEAURAINVILLE	22-12-16		RH RP&B as 15-12-16 1 Pair & D. Horses + 1 Driver to 8th Cav Bde	
			1LD Horse + 1 Driver from 8th	
			Railhead & Refilling Point MARESQUEL Billets BEAURAINVILLE	
do	23-12-16		RH RP&B as 22-12-16	
do	24-12-16		RH RP&B as 22-12-16. 1 team of Coy. 1 team of Res Pk from 7th Cav Bde. 1 Driver from Hospital	
do	25-12-16		RH RP&B as 22-12-16	
do	26-12-16		RH RP&B as 22-12-16	
do	27-12-16		RH RP&B as 22-12-16	

C.P. Moeller. Capt.
O.C. 3rd Cav. Div. Qua H.T.Co

WAR DIARY
or
INTELLIGENCE SUMMARY.
(Erase heading not required.)

Army Form C. 2118.

Place	Date	Hour	Summary of Events and Information	Remarks and references to Appendices
BEAURAINVILLE			Railhead + Refilling Point MARESQUEL Billets BEAURAINVILLE.	
do	29/12/16		2 LD horses Cast to No 20 MVS. (No 35+99)	
do	30/12/16		2 LD horses attached from Bde H.Q to No 20 M.V.S.	
			R.H. RP&B as 28-12-16.	
			R.H. RP&B as 28-12-16. 1 Driver to Hospital	
			Capt Buckley A.S.C. Reported for Duty from B.H.T.D. Coy	
do	31-12-16		R.H. RP&B as 28-12-16. Inspection of Coy horses and 5th Reserve Park horses by V.O. 13th M.V.S.	

C.J.Butler Capt.
O.C. 3rd Cav. Div. Aux. H.T. Co.

WAR DIARY or INTELLIGENCE SUMMARY

Army Form C. 2118.

Place	Date	Hour	Summary of Events and Information	Remarks and references to Appendices
BEAURAINVILLE	1/1/17		Relleva & Refilling Point MARESQUEL BILLETS BEAURAINVILLE No. 74/65-8676 7/c/cpl RIDLEY W.S. appointed T/S/C with pay 7/11/16.	
do	2/1/17		1 L.D. Horse 5th Cav Reserve Park to M.V.S. (No 13) Capt W.N. BUCKLEY resumed command of the Coy from Capt C.F.K. WELLER R.H.R.P.& B as 1/1/17. 1 Driver to hospital	
do	3/1/17		R.H.R.P.& B as 1/1/17. Capt C.F.R. WELLER proceeds to M.T. School of Instr on transfer	
do	4/1/17		R.H.R.P.& B as 1/1/17. 2 men leave to U.K. till 14/1/17	
do	5/1/17		R.H.R.P.& B as 1/1/17. { 1 Driver to Hospital 26 Jan 10th { 1 L.D. Horse evacuated from 20 M.V.S. 1 Driver to Hospital 26 Jan 30 K.	
do	6/1/17		R.H.R.P.& B as 1/1/17. 2 L.D. horses from Park. 1 L.D. to H.Q. Cav. Bde.	
do	7/1/17		R.H.R.P.& B as 1/1/17. 1 O/C from H.Q. 7 Bde 2 Gra. from D.R.S.	
do	8/1/17		R.H.R.P.& B as 1/1/17. Civic PEARLESS 1 S/C 1 cycle 2 Drivers 3 riding horses of 5 Car. Res. Park to detachment with 3 Cav. Ammn Park 1 L.D. horse to No 13 Mob.Vet. Sec.	
do	9/1/17		R.H.R.P.& B as 1/1/17. 1 Gr. to Hospital 1 R. Capt. BUCKLEY inspects transport with 6th Bde. S.S.M. HOLT and 1 Driver from 3 Cav. Ammn. Park. 1 R. horse from 3 Cav. Ammn. Park. 70th Buckley Capt. O.C. 3 Cav Div. AuxLH.T.Coy	

A.D.S.S./Forms/C. 2118.

WAR DIARY or INTELLIGENCE SUMMARY

Army Form C. 2118.

Place	Date	Hour	Summary of Events and Information	Remarks and references to Appendices
BOURAINVILLE 10/1/17			Railhead and Refilling Point MARESQUEL Billets BEAURAINVILLE	
			1 Driver to Hospital	
do	11/1/17		R.H.R.P.B as 10/1/17	
do	12/1/17		R.H.R.P.B as 10/1/17	
do	13/1/17		Railhead and Refilling Point BEAURAINVILLE Billets BEAURAINVILLE	
			2 L.D. horses evacuated to 20 M.V.S. CAPT MM BUCKLEY to hospital & attached to 7th Bde.	
			5 teams 3rd Car R.P. changed with detach. 3rd Amm. Park.	1/L CAPT M.M.BUCKLEY inspected 11/1/17. Transfer with 7th Bde. CAPT M.M. BUCKLEY to hospital. Attached with 7 Bde.
do	14/1/17		R.H.R.P.B as 13/1/17	
			1 L.D. horse from No 13 M.V.S. (not struck off)	
			Inspection of animals of Coy and 5th Reserve Park	
			by V.O. 13th M.V.S.	
do	15/1/17		R.H.R.P.B as 13/1/17	
			1 Sub. R.F.A. from Base Dep. ℅ 137th	
			2 L.D. evacuated from A. Coy's 26/12/16	
			2 L.D. evacuated from A. Coy's 10/1/16	
			1 L.D. evacuated from Cav. Corps 1/1/17	
do	16/1/17		R.H.R.P.B as 13/1/17	
do	17/1/17		R.H.R.P.B as 13/1/17	

T.N.Dalby Capt
O.C. 3rd Cav. Bre. Aux. H.T. Coy.

Army Form C. 2118.

WAR DIARY
or
INTELLIGENCE SUMMARY.
(Erase heading not required.)

Instructions regarding War Diaries and Intelligence Summaries are contained in F. S. Regs., Part II. and the Staff Manual respectively. Title pages will be prepared in manuscript.

Place	Date	Hour	Summary of Events and Information	Remarks and references to Appendices
BEAURAINVILLE	18/1/17		Railhead & Refilling Point BEAURAINVILLE Billets BEAURAINVILLE 3 Sto. leave to U.K. till 28/1/17. Medical inspection by M.O.	
do	19/1/17		R.H.R.P and B as 18/1/17 CAPT. W.N. BUCKLEY inspected Transport (with 5th Bde.	
do	20/1/17		R.H.R.P and B as 18/1/17. 3 Sto. to Brtash. Stockn. RES. PARK at 3rd CAV. AMM. PARK.	
do	21/1/17		R.H.R.P and B as 18/1/17. 1ST. R.H.Q. 7 Cav. Bde. CPL. HE. PARKHOUSE to Hosp 16/17.	
do	22/1/17		R.H.R.P and B as 18/1/17. 1ST Scav. Res. Park to R.H.Q. 7th Cav. Bde. 1ST. 2 L.D. horses to N.S.Y.	
do	23/1/17		R.H.R.P and B as 18/1/17. H.Q. of Coy moved from BEAURAINVILLE to LESPINOY. 2 L.D. horses evacuated by N.S.I. 14/12/16. 1 L.D. to 10th Hussars. 1 L.D. from 10th Hussars to R.H.Q.L. 1 L.D. from R.H.G.D. 6.H.Q.C. of Coy.	
LESPINOY	24/1/17		Railhead & Refilling Point BEAURAINVILLE Billets LESPINOY 3 Sto. leave to U.K. till 4/2/17 (4 2/17)	
do	25/1/17		RHRP & B as 24/1/17	
do	26/1/17		RHRP & B as 24/1/17	
do	27/1/17		RHRP & B as 24/1/17	

W.N. Buckley Capt
O.C. 3rd Cav. Div. Supr. H.T. Coy.

WAR DIARY
or
INTELLIGENCE SUMMARY.

(Erase heading not required.)

Army Form C. 2118.

Place	Date	Hour	Summary of Events and Information	Remarks and references to Appendices
LESPINOY	28/1/17		Railhead & Refilling Point BEAURAINVILLE Billets LESPINOY. w/c McDougall 4 S.O. 8 L.D. 1 wagon to base Rly syc NEUFCHATEL for duty.	
do	29/1/17		R.H.R.P. & B. as 28/1/17. 2 S.O. & 4 mules to Base Veterinary. 1 S.O. & Detachmt of Billets L-Day L.Don from 3rd A.D.M.S.	
do	30/1/17		R.H.R.P. & B. as 28/1/17. 3 S.O. 4 L.D. horses, 1 wagon from B.T.O.J. to Cav. Depot (att. from S. Cav. Bn. Park) 5 Off. 12 O.R. 19 horses billetted for night and 1 due returns.	
do	31/1/17		R.H.R.P. & B. as 28/1/17. 1 S.S. 3 S.S. 4 horses 1 wagon to S. Cav. Bn. Park. to detach 3 Cav. Amm. Park.	

W.N. Buckley Capt.
O.C., 3rd Cav. Fld. Amb. M.T. Coy.

WAR DIARY or INTELLIGENCE SUMMARY

Army Form C. 2118.

Place	Date	Hour	Summary of Events and Information	Remarks and references to Appendices
LESPINOY	1/2/17		Railway Refilling Point BEAURAINVILLE Billets LESPINOY	
			3 OR. leave to U.K. till 11/2/17.	
			1 OR. R.F.A. to Hospital 22/7.	
			2 Off. 27 OR. and 31 horses billeted for night and 2 days rations.	
do	2/2/17		R.H.R.P. 1/S as 1/2/17. C/S McDougall & S/S Shores from Tot as 1/C NEUFCHATEL	
do	3/2/17		R.H.R.P. - B as 1/2/17. A/Cpl F.N. Bailey 7 pl. W.S. Ridley to 6th rate Cpl. Pay [from 29/11/16]	
			C.O.2 of 19/17	
do	4/2/17		R.H.R.P. - B as 1/2/17. Sr W. Gillham appointed 0/0pe with pay 7/6.	
			Inspection of all animals by V.O. 13 M.V.S.	
do	5/2/17		R.H.R.P. - B as 1/2/17.	
do	6/2/17		R.H.R.P. - B as 1/2/17. 0/nsh. Cpl. Childwick. S.S. Williams R.C. to Div.Wk.Shop CONTES.	
do	7/2/17		R.H.R.P. - B as 1/2/17. SR/23 A/pl/Sergt Haines I.N. granted pay of rank 26/7.	
do	8/2/17		R.H.R.P. - B as 1/2/17. A/Cpl King H. leave to U.K. till 8/3/17. 2 OR. leave to U.K. till 18/2/17.	
			From Canvey from B.S.S. Cav. Res. Park. 1 Dr. S. Rea. Park to 10 Hussars.	
			1 Dr. to P.R.D	
			Medical Inspection by M.O. Yc.	
			W.N. Pierce	
			Capt & 0/3 525 Cav.Fd.Amb. T.Coy	

WAR DIARY or INTELLIGENCE SUMMARY

Army Form C. 2118.

Place	Date	Hour	Summary of Events and Information	Remarks and references to Appendices
LESPINOY	9/2/17		Railhead & Refilling Point BEAURAINVILLE. Billets LESPINOY.	
do	10/2/17		R.H.R.P. & B. as 9/2/17. 1 Dr. special leave. Lynskope C. Shewin R. granted 15y of June 9/9/17	
do	11/2/17		R.H.R.P. & B. as 9/2/17. Animal inspection by V.O. c/c.	
do	12/2/17		R.H.R.P. & B. as 9/2/17. 1 Sr. to 2 Life Guards. 1 Dr. from 2 Life Guards.	
do	13/2/17		R.H.R.P. & B. as 9/2/17. 1 Sr. (R.H.A.) from Cav. Corps. 2 Srs. 1 team 1 wagon from 7 Cav. Bde. c/c Hall from St. S. Cav. Res. Park.	
do	14/2/17		R.H.R.P. & B. as 9/2/17. 1 Sr. to Cav. Corps.	
do	15/2/17		R.H.R.P. & B. as 9/2/17. 2 Srs. 5 L.D. to Cav. Corps. 2 Drs. 4 mules to 15th Hussars for duty. 2 Srs. 4 L.D. from R.H.Cg. Medical Inspection by M.O.	
do	16/2/17		R.H.R.P. & B. as 9/2/17.	
do	17/2/17		R.H.R.P. & B. as 9/2/17. 1 Dr. from Div. H.P.	
do	18/2/17		R.H.R.P. & B. as 9/2/17. Inspection of animals by C.O. 2 Drs. 4 L.D. 1 mule 5 Cav. Res. Park from 7 Cav. Bde. 1 Dr. from J.P.	
do	19/2/17		R.H.R.P. & B. as 9/2/17. 1 Dr. to R.H.Cg. for duty. 1 L.D. to R.H.Cg. 1 Dr. from Cav. Corps.	
do	20/2/17		R.H.R.P. & B. as 9/2/17.	
do	21/2/17		R.H.R.P. & B. as 9/2/17. 2 Drs. from 3rd D.G. 1 L.D. home with 10th Hussars. 1 L.D. Hussars died. T.O.M. Buckley Capt. & adj. 3rd Cav. Bri. Aux. H.T. Coy.	

Army Form C. 2118.

WAR DIARY
or
INTELLIGENCE SUMMARY.
(Erase heading not required.)

Instructions regarding War Diaries and Intelligence Summaries are contained in F. S. Regs., Part II. and the Staff Manual respectively. Title pages will be prepared in manuscript.

Place	Date	Hour	Summary of Events and Information	Remarks and references to Appendices
LESPINOY	22/2/17		Railhead & Refilling Point BEAURAINVILLE Billets LESPINOY. a/Cpl McDougall, R.A.M.C. o/c A/Cpl with Pay 16/1/17. Auth. A.S.C. S.R.P.6/259 8/12/19. A/Cpl McDougall R. to 6th rate Cpls Pay 16/2/17. Medical inspection by M.O.	
do	23/2/17		R.H.R.P. & B as 22/2/17. 1 Dr to Det. 5 Cav. Res. Park at 3 Armee Park. 1 Dr from Det 5 Cav Res. Park at 3 Cayeux Park.	
do	24/2/17		R.H.R.P. & B as 22/2/17. 1 Dr to 1st R.D.	
do	25/2/17		R.H.R.P. & B as 22/2/17. Inspection of all animals by V.O. 1 Dr from 1st R.D.	
do	26/2/17		R.H.R.P. & B as 22/2/17. Tpr. Heron leave 11/2/17 to 24/2/17.	
do	27/2/17		R.H.R.P. & B as 22/2/17. 1 Dr to R.A.C.9 for duty. 1 Dr from leave to Det. 5 Cav R.P. 1 Dr to N.S.Y.	
do	28/2/17		R.H.R.P. & B as 22/2/17. 1 Dr from 5th Cav.Res. Park from N.S.Y. CAPT W.N.BUCKLEY to GAS SCHOOL, WAILLY.	

W.N. Buckley Capt G
aux H.T. Coy

O/C 3rd Cav Bde. aux H.T. Coy

WAR DIARY
or
INTELLIGENCE SUMMARY.

(Erase heading not required).

Army Form C. 2118.

Aux HT Coy

Place	Date	Hour	Summary of Events and Information	Remarks and references to Appendices
LESPINOY	1/3/17		Railhead & Refilling Point BEAURAINVILLE B.U.6. LESPINOY.	
do	2/3/17		R.H.R.P. & B. as 1/3/17. 3 Drs from HQ 5 Cav. Res. Park.	
do	3/3/17		R.H.R.P. & B. as 1/3/17. HQ of Coy moved from LESPINOY to ST. DENOEUX. CAPT W.N. BUCKLEY from GAS SCHOOL, WAILLY.	
ST. DENOEUX	4/3/17		R.H.R.P. & BEAURAINVILLE B.U.6. ST. DENOEUX.	
do	5/3/17		R.H.R.P. & B. as 4/3/17. 2 Drs left Det. with 3rd Cav.Sn. Ammn Park. 1 Dr to 1st R.D.	
do	6/3/17		R.H.R.P. & B. as 4/3/17. 1 Dr from 1st R.D. 1 L.D. & Res. Park to 10 Hussars. 1 L.D. Coy. from 10 Hussars.	
do	7/3/17		R.H.R.P. B. as 4/3/17. 1 Dr. to 2nd L.G. 1 Dr. 5 Cav. R.P. to 3rd Ammn. Pk. Detail. Dr. Keeley T.H. R.F.A. to Lt II. Prof. Pay @ 3d from 12.17. (A.C.I. 2441 d/28/7/16.) Mash./Cpl. Chidwick R. to 5th Rate of Coys Pay 9d/17. Inspection of transport at Railhead by A.D. of S.T.C.C. 1 Dr. to D.R.S.	
do	8/3/17		R.H.R.P. B as 4/3/17.	
do	9/3/17		R.H.R.P. B as 4/3/17.	
do	10/3/17		R.H.R.P. B as 4/3/17. 1 Pte to 10th Hussars. 1 Dr from 10th Hussars. 1 L.D. horse evacuated by 1st L.G. on 3/17. { 1 L.D. horse aux Coy destroyed } with Cinicto Veo. 5/17. 1 Dr. 5 Cav. Res. Park to Hoof. 1 Dr. 3rd Cav. Sn Aux H.T Coy. 70/N.Buckley/capt ally 3rd Cav Sn aux HT Coy	

WAR DIARY or INTELLIGENCE SUMMARY

Army Form C. 2118.

Place	Date	Hour	Summary of Events and Information	Remarks and references to Appendices
ST. DENOEUX	11/3/17		Railhead & Refilling Point BEAURAINVILLE Billets ST. DENOEUX.	
do	12/3/17		RHRP & B as 11/3/17. Inspection of animals by V.O. in charge.	
do	13/3/17		RHRP & B as 11/3/17. Inspection by A.D.V.S. 3rd Cav. Div.	
do	14/3/17		RHRP & B as 11/3/17. 1 Ride H. from 8th Bde. HQ. 1 Dr from 8th Bde H.Q. Medical Inspection by M.O.	
do	15/3/17		RHRP & B as 11/3/17. 1 L.D. horse from 10th N. (5th Cav. R.P.) 1 L.D. horse 5th Cav. R.P. to 10th H.	
No	15/3/17		RHRP & B as 11/3/17. 2 L.D. horses (5th Cav R.P.) to 1st S.G. 1 L.D. horse (5th Cav R.P.) from 1st S.G.	
do	16/3/17		RHRP & B as 11/3/17. 1 Major G.S. & L.D. horses 2 Drs. from 8 M.G.S. 1 Major G.S. T/22606 A/C/C Ray) S. 5th Cav. R.P. deptd. See Pack 2 D.D from 5th Cav. R.P.	
do	17/3/17		RHRP & B as 11/3/17.	
do	18/3/17		RHRP & B as 11/3/17. C. of E. Parade 10.15 a.m.	
do	19/3/17		RHRP & B as 11/3/17. 1 R. 16 L.D. horses 4 mules S majors G.S. Inter cart 1 Sadd S. 1 Wh. 1 Dmr. 18 R. & F. to O.C. 5th S. Cav. R.P. BEAURAINVILLE 2 L.D. horses for casting from O/C 5/C 5 Cav. Rn. Park.	
do	20/3/17		RHRP & B as 11/3/17. Det. 5th Cav. Res. Park as for B 213 A ceases to be attacked. 3 L.D. Coy. 6 L.D. 5th Cav. R.P. to 13 M.V.S. for casting 7 L.D. horses to 5th Cav. Rn. Park. 4 L. D mules to 5th Cav. Rn. Park. 3 teams from 10th Hussars.	

N.J. Buckley Capt E
adj 3rd Cav Div. Rest H.T. Coy.

WAR DIARY
or
INTELLIGENCE SUMMARY.
(Erase heading not required.)

Army Form C. 2118.

Place	Date	Hour	Summary of Events and Information	Remarks and references to Appendices
ST. DENOEUX	21/3/17		Railhead & Refilling Point BEAURAINVILLE Billets ST DENOEUX. 4 trams from Bury Yeo. 3 trams from R.H Guard.	
do	22/3/17		R H R P & B as 21/3/17. 1 tram from "G" By R.H.A. {1 Div.}1 Asst cart & team from A.H.T.D ABEVILLE. Lecture & inspection by M.O.	
do	23/3/17		R H R P & B as 21/3/17. 1 L.D. horse died. 1 Cpl. 1 C/C. & 4 DYs from Base H.T. Y.C.R. {2 Div} to the 2 Sn Sqdn, 2 DVs 1 Div. Maint. & & to H.C. 6 Br.R.	
do	24/3/17		R H R P & B as 21/3/17. Horse & Harness inspection.	
do	25/3/17		R H R P & B as 21/3/17. Wagon & equipment inspection.	
do	26/3/17		R H R P & B as 21/3/17. 1 Dr. to A.R.S.	
do	27/3/17		R H R P & B as 21/3/17. 2 Lt. C.H. SENDELL 3 N.C.O.s, 1 Farr. 23 Sys. & 3 horses to BEAURAINVILLE for temp. duty.	
do	28/3/17		R H R P & B as 21/3/17.	
do	29/3/17		R H R P & B as 21/3/17. 1 L.D. horse to 3 D.Cy. Rifle & smoke helmet inspection. No 24720 Dr. Knight W. to A.P.M. 3 Cav Div.	
do	30/3/17		R H R P & B as 21/3/17. S.B.R. fitted by D.G.O.	
do	31/3/17		R H R P & B as 21/3/17. Sergt. Graham 2nd Cpl. Walker Cpl. Ridley 18 Drs. 2 R. 20 L.D. horses 12 mules from Cav. Corps.	

T.T. Buckley Capt.
O/C 3rd Cav. Bn. Aux. H.T. Cy.

WAR DIARY or INTELLIGENCE SUMMARY

Army Form C. 2118.

Place	Date	Hour	Summary of Events and Information	Remarks and references to Appendices
ST.DENOEUX	1/4/17		Railhead and Refilling Point BEAURAINVILLE Billets ST.DENOEUX. 2 St.C.H. SENDELL 3 N.C.Os 17mn. 2 D'rs. 43 L.D. from BEAURAINVILLE	
do	2/4/17		R.H.R.P.v.B as 1/4/17. 1 Dr to No 26 Gen.H.	
do	3/4/17		R.H.R.P.v.B as 1/4/17. 5 Drs from Base Depot. 1 Sergt v 7 teams complete to VI Bde. 1 team v Cpl. to 7 Bde H.Q. 1 Sergt 13 teams to 8th Bde. 1 Off. 1 Pvt. S.S. 27mn. 2 wh. 2 sadd. 62 R.+ 7 from 10th Res Pk. attached (with limbers) for rations. 3 Drs (6 N° 20 Gen H.P.	
do	4/4/17.		R.H.R.P.v.B as 1/4/17. 1 Dr R.F.A. to 26 Gen I.P. 1 C/c to Base S/of A.S.C. 1 Dr R.F.A. to Base depot R.F.A. 24 L.D. mules from Base. 1 L.D. mule to 13 M.K.S.	
do	5/4/17.		R.H.R.P.v.B as 1/4/17. 3 S.D. from Base Depot.	
do	6/4/17		R.H.R.P.v.B as 1/4/17.	
do	7/4/17.		R.H.R.P.v.B as 1/4/17. Coy. move from ST.DENOEUX to MONCHEL.	
MONCHEL	8/4/17		Dunn to MONCHEL 1 Dr to Leicester Yeo. 1 Off. 17mn.S.S. 2 hrs. 2 wh. 3 Sad. 62R.&7 from 10th R.P. attached. Coy move from MONCHEL to BOUBERS SUR CONCHE. 38 Wagons of teams rejoined from Units. 38 wagons bringt. Ammn. Park with Ammunition. 2 Drs from Leicester Yeo.	W.S.P. Pucklev Capt. O/c 3 Car Div Auxx H.T. Coy

Army Form C. 2118.

WAR DIARY
or
INTELLIGENCE SUMMARY.
(Erase heading not required.)

Instructions regarding War Diaries and Intelligence Summaries are contained in F. S. Regs., Part II. and the Staff Manual respectively. Title pages will be prepared in manuscript.

Place	Date	Hour	Summary of Events and Information	Remarks and references to Appendices
BOUBERS SUR CONCHE	8/4/17		Dump N BOUBERS SUR CONCHE Billets BOUBERS SUR CONCHE 3 Drs to IP.	
do	10/4/17		Do Bas 9/4/17. Coy moved from BOUBERS to ETREE-WAMIN 1 Dr to RH RFA Bde.	
ETREE WAMIN	11/4/17		Dump and Billets ETREE WAMIN. Coy moved from ETREE WAMIN to FOSSEUX 1 LD horse 1 LD mule evacuated.	
FOSSEUX	12/4/17		Coy moved from FOSSEUX to ETREE WAMIN.	
ETREE WAMIN	13/4/17		Dump and Billets ETREE WAMIN. 1 LD horse died.	
do	14/4/17		D and B as 13/4/17. 1 Dr to IP.	
do	15/4/17		D and B as 13/4/17. 3 L.D. horses from Base Remounts. Part of Amm. return taken.	
do	16/4/17		D and B as 13/4/17. amm. loads shifted.	
do	17/4/17		D and B as 13/4/17. 1 L.D. horse died.	
do	18/4/17		D and B as 13/4/17. Mending other parade.	
do	19/4/17		D and B as 13/4/17.	
do	20/4/17		D and B as 13/4/17. Coy. moved from ETREE-WAMIN to REGNAUVILLE	
REGNAUVILLE	21/4/17		Dump & Billets REGNAUVILLE. 2 Drs from IP. 2 Drs from 6th Bde K.L. dism. half. 1 tank G.S. wagon 2 horses from 6 Bde K.C. dism. half. 1 wagon team from Divn Sup. Tn Packedey Cafe. Amm returned from wagon Park. cct 4 3 Lewis Gun XXX LCH	

WAR DIARY or INTELLIGENCE SUMMARY

Army Form C. 2118.

Place	Date	Hour	Summary of Events and Information	Remarks and references to Appendices
REGNAUVILLE	22/4/17		Dump r Billets REGNAUVILLE Railed BEAURAINVILLE. 1 Sgt. 1 Cpl. 1 Fm. 1 Shoemk. 36 team wagons. 72 ers to Units of Div.	
do	23/4/17		D. B. R as 22/4/17.	
do	24/4/17		D. B. R as 22/4/17.	
do	25/4/17		A B.R as 22/4/17. Inspection of horses. 1 Dr from R.	
do	26/4/17		D.B.R as 22/4/17. 1 Pte to No.7 F.A. Recv'd 776247 a/ldr to Sh Methwick H.	
do	27/4/17		D B.R as 22/4/17. 1 Tpr. to No.7 F.A. Inspection of transport by O.C. A.T.C. 3 Cav Bri. 1 Dr from R. 3 L.D. horses 2 L.D. mules to No.14 M.V.S. 1 sr to R.	
do	28/4/17		A B.R as 22/4/17. 1 Dr to R. 1 sr to No.7 C.T.A.	
do	29/4/17		A B.R as 22/4/17.	
do	30/4/17		A B.R as 22/4/17. 1 Dr to No.7 C.T.A. 3 srs from B.H.T.D.	To W. Buckley Capt Rex H.T. Coy O/c 3 Cav.Bri.

WAR DIARY or INTELLIGENCE SUMMARY

Army Form C. 2118.

3 Cdn H.T. Coy

Place	Date	Hour	Summary of Events and Information	Remarks
REGNAUVILLE	1/5/17		Billets REGNAUVILLE. 1 Dr. to 7th C.F.A.	
do	2/5/17		Billets as 1/5/17. 1 Scout from 7th C.F.A.	
do	3/5/17		Billets as 1/5/17. 2 Drs to H.P. 1 Dr to H.P. 26/4/17	
do	4/5/17		Billets as 1/5/17.	
do	5/5/17		Billets as 1/5/17.	
do	6/5/17		Billets as 1/5/17. 1 Dr from 7th C.F.A. 1 Sr. from Base Depot. 1 Dr to 7th C.F.A. Church Parade	
do	7/5/17		Billets as 1/5/17. 1 Dr from 7th C.F.A. 1 Dr to 8th Bde HQ. 1 L.D. cas it to No 14 M.V.S. 1 Dr from H.P.	
do	8/5/17		Billets as 1/5/17. Sr. Dent Special leave to U.K. 10th to 20th	
do	9/5/17		Billets as 1/5/17. 1 Dr to 6th Cav Bde to relieve Sr Dent.	
do	10/5/17		Billets as 1/5/17. 1 Sgt. 1 Farr. 1 Cpl. 6 trans + 13 Drs from Cav. Corps. 1 Dr. to H.P. 1 Dr. R.F.A. to H.P.	
do	11/5/17		Billets as 1/5/17. Harness inspection. 5 teams + Drs. to 7th Cav Bde. 5 teams + Drs to 8th Cav Bde.	

P/A/ Sgt. McIntosh G. from No 2 Vet. H.P. 1 Dr from R.H.9

W.N. Brackley Capt
O.C. 3 Car Bri Cav H.T. Co.

WAR DIARY
or
INTELLIGENCE SUMMARY.

(Erase heading not required.)

Army Form C. 2118.

Instructions regarding War Diaries and Intelligence Summaries are contained in F. S. Regs. Part II. and the Staff Manual respectively. Title pages will be prepared in manuscript.

Place	Date	Hour	Summary of Events and Information	Remarks and references to Appendices
REGNAUVILLE	11/5/17		Billets REGNAUVILLE. 1 Dr. R.F.A. to H.R. 1 Dr. to 3RD D.G.	
do	12/5/17		Billets as 11/5/17. SR/23 A/Sgt. Haines I.N. A/C. reverted to Cpl.	
			SR/23 C/Cpl. Haines I.N. A/C. to No. 2 Vet. H.	
do	13/5/17		HQ of Coy marched from REGNAUVILLE to WAVANS.	
WAVANS	14/5/17		HQ of Coy marched from WAVANS to TALMAS.	
TALMAS	15/5/17		HQ of Coy marched from TALMAS to QUERRIEU.	
QUERRIEU	16/5/17		Billets QUERRIEU.	
QUERRIEU	17/5/17		HQ of Coy marched from QUERRIEU to LAMOTTE.	
LAMOTTE	18/5/17		Billets LAMOTTE. Gas Box Respirator and drill by D.G.O.	
LAMOTTE	19/5/17		HQ of Coy marched from LAMOTTE to COURCELLES. Encamped in field Ref map. 62C. J 33 C.2.7 min to J 33. B.5.3. south of road N of wood.	
COURCELLES	20/5/17		Laying out of camp. Railway PLAMICOURT.	
COURCELLES	21/5/17		Good district for grazing.	
do	22/5/17		2 Drs. from Base Depot.	
do	23/5/17		1 L.D. horse destroyed at 14 M.V.S. Full marching order parade and S.B.R. drill.	
			TS/4485. Farr. W. Winnins R. leave to U.K. 24/5/17 to 3/6/17.	
do	24/5/17		Inspection of kit. 7/Ct. C.H. SENDELL to ENGLAND for transfer to R.F.A. Subject to passing course.	

707 N. Buckley Capt.
O/g. 3 Cav. Div. Aux. H.T. Coy.

WAR DIARY
or
INTELLIGENCE SUMMARY.
(Erase heading not required.)

Army Form C. 2118.

Place	Date	Hour	Summary of Events and Information	Remarks and references to Appendices
COURCELLES	25/5/17		2 Drs. with steam & Tank wagon to Div. H.Q. (advanced)	
do	26/5/17		Railhead removed from FLAMICOURT to TINCOURT.	
do	27/5/17		Inspection of harness. T/2/Lt. T.E.W.D. SIMPSON from Base Depot for duty	
do	28/5/17		Full marching order parade. S.B.R. inspection & drill.	
do	29/5/17		Bathing parade at TINCOURT.	
do	30/5/17			
do	31/5/17		2 Drs. to 8th C.F.A.	

T.V. Buckley Capt
O/C 2nd Aus. Div. M.T. Coy

WAR DIARY or INTELLIGENCE SUMMARY.

Army Form C. 2118.

3 Cav Aux H.T Coy

Vol 17

Place	Date	Hour	Summary of Events and Information	Remarks and references to Appendices
COURCELLES	1/6/17		Railhead TINCOURT.	
do	2/6/17		do	
do	3/6/17		do Harness inspection. 1 Dr from 8th C.T.A	
do	4/6/17		do Fell marching order hunt & gas drill	
do	5/6/17		do Inspection of 6th Cav Bde Transport (H.T.Coy) Visit of Inspector of Food Economies	
do	6/6/17		do Inspection of 7th Cav Bde. Transport (H.T.Coy)	
do	7/6/17		do Inspection of 8th Cav Bde Transport (H.T.Coy) 1 Dr "C" Battery to relieve Dr Metcalfe. No T/1765 Farr. Cpl. "/Farr. Sergt ALLEN W. promoted Farr. Sergt. 5/3/17. T/17091 Cpl. "/Sergt HUGHES. T. promoted Sergt. 5/3/17. T/27300 Cpl. "/Sergt GRAHAM W. promoted Cpl. 5/3/17. Corps order 49 d 17/4/17	F.R. Buckley Lt a/g 3 Cav. Div. Aux H.T. Coy

Army Form C. 2118.

WAR DIARY
or
INTELLIGENCE SUMMARY.
(Erase heading not required.)

Place	Date	Hour	Summary of Events and Information	Remarks and references to Appendices
COURCELLES	8/6/17		Railhead TINCOURT.	
do	9/6/17		do 6 teams & wagons w/ 1 N.C.O. returned from each Bty.	
do	10/6/17		do 29050 Dr METCALFE J. leave to U.K. 16 Syts 20 men	
			2/Lt T.E.W. DAWES SIMPSON 2 Sngts 2 Cpls 2 Drvrs	
			35 R.T. 4 Riding 15 teams & wagons to 30 Bri K.C.	
do	11/6/17		do for duty.	
			Dr. GUSTARD R: 21 days F.P. No. 1.	
do	12/6/17		do Dr. OATS W. 7 days F.P. No 2	
do	13/6/17		do Dr. MUNGE S.L. from Base B.p.O.C.	
do	14/6/17		do Marching order & gas drill. Dr. Waters from P.	
			1 team from new B.C.	
do	15/6/17		do F.S.M. HOLT C. to Abv. K.C.	
			Dr. Bolophie do	
			Drvr. Williams do	
			Drvr. Cornish from new K.C. 757 Pr Bradley to Col.	
			Sgt 3 Can Div Amm. A.T. Col.	

Army Form C. 2118.

WAR DIARY
or
INTELLIGENCE SUMMARY.
(Erase heading not required.)

Place	Date	Hour	Summary of Events and Information	Remarks and references to Appendices
COURCELLES	16/6/17		Railhead TINCOURT.	
do	17/6/17		do Harness Inspection 3 squ. Hosp	
			Lt Col. Shine from A.d.H.Q. St Mungo S.C. & Smar Sea	
do	18/6/17		do P.U. marching order inspection no. 9 or Still.	
			Capt W.N. BUCKLEY leave to U.K. 20/6/17 to 30/6/17	
do	19/6/17		do 13 mules from Base Remounts	
do	20/6/17		do St Seuringh leave to U.K. 21/6/17 to 1/7/17	
do	21/6/17		do	
do	22/6/17		do	
do	23/6/17		do	
do	24/6/17		do	
do	25/6/17		do P.U. marching order inspection & gas drill. A.G.L.H.P.247	
do	26/6/17		do	
do	27/6/17		do St. Curtis J. from Base 3/7/17 (H.T.S.)	
do	28/6/17		do St. H. Scamble Z. leave to U.K. 28/6/17 to 8/7/17	
do	29/6/17		do 1 mule evacuated to No 20 M.V.S.	
			St. Amore Corbin 2/Lt. Te M.D SIMPSON returned to A.A.C.	
			10. M.D Buckley C.A.F.C.	

Army Form C. 2118.

WAR DIARY
or
INTELLIGENCE SUMMARY.

(Erase heading not required.)

Instructions regarding War Diaries and Intelligence Summaries are contained in F. S. Regs., Part II. and the Staff Manual respectively. Title pages will be prepared in manuscript.

Place	Date	Hour	Summary of Events and Information	Remarks and references to Appendices
COURCELLES	30/6/17		Railhead TINCOURT.	

W.M. Blakey / Capt
adj. 2nd A. Div. Sup. Col. M.T. Coy.

2353 Wt. W2544/1454 700,000 5/15 D. D. & L. A.D.S.S./Forms/C. 2118.

Army Form C. 2118

WAR DIARY
or
INTELLIGENCE SUMMARY
(Erase heading not required.)

Vol 18

Place	Date	Hour	Summary of Events and Information	Remarks and references to Appendices
COURCELLES	1/7/17		Railhead TINCOURT. Sgt Stevens & 3 teams to 8th Bde. Sgt Graham & 6 teams to 7th Bde. Cpl. Parkinson 6 teams to 6th Bde. Sto. Blyther Metcalfe 1 team to Essex Yeo. Sto. Ball & Boyd & 3 horses from Essex Yeo. 1 mule changed for Essex Yeo.	
– do –	2/7/17		Railhead as 1/7/17. Lt. Philipps R.H. to H.	
– do –	3/7/17		Railhead as 1/7/17. HQ of Coy moved from COURCELLES to FLAMICOURT. Lt. Crean N.R. evacuated sick. Lt. Matthews P.H. & P 29/6/17. Sto. Brown 2/C. & P 29/6/17. Sto. Mystery J. Brown A.M.T. & H.	
FLAMICOURT	4/7/17		HQ of Coy moved from FLAMICOURT to TREUX. Lt. Screen R.F leave to U.K. 5 to 15/7.	
TREUX	5/7/17.		HQ of Coy moved from TREUX to DOULLENS.	
DOULLENS	6/7/17.		HQ of Coy moved from DOULLENS to SAINS. (Nr St POL)	
SAINS	7/7/17.		HQ of Coy moved from SAINS to PERNES.	
PERNES	8/7/17.		Sto. Davies A.M.T. Matthews R. from H. W.N. Pinckney Capt dy 3 Cav. Bn. Res. H.T. Coy.	

Army Form C. 2118

WAR DIARY
or
INTELLIGENCE SUMMARY
(Erase heading not required.)

Instructions regarding War Diaries and Intelligence Summaries are contained in F. S. Regs, Part II. and the Staff Manual respectively. Title Pages will be prepared in manuscript.

Place	Date	Hour	Summary of Events and Information	Remarks and references to Appendices
PERNES	9/7/17	Dump	PERNES. Full marching order parade. Gas drill and inspection of helmets.	
do	10/7/17	Dump	as 9/7/17.	
do	11/7/17	Dump	as 9/7/17. Inspection of harness.	
do	12/7/17	Dump	as 9/7/17. Inspection of kit.	
do	13/7/17	Dump	as 9/7/17. S. Smith. Walker H. to Div. H.Q. for temp duty. Drs. Boyd & Pord with team to 10th Hussars. Ptes. Hultain & Cavanagh from 10th Hussars with 3 horses.	
do	14/7/17	Dump	as 9/7/17. St. Barwick to "K" Batty.	
do	15/7/17	Dump	as 9/7/17. HQ moved from PERNES to BUSNES.	
do	16/7/17	Dump	as 9/7/17. Tpr. Neale from I.C.G. St. Seringill to I.C.G. St. Allan to H.Q. 7 Bde. St. Lawrence from H.Q. 7 Bde.	
BUSNES	17/7/17	Dump	BUSNES Railway ARE Tpr. Neale W. St. Lockerby J. St. Lawrence J.? leave to U.K. till 27/7/17. Marching order parade. Gas drill	

L/N. Buckley Capt
dcg 3 Cav. Div. Aux. H.T.Coy.

WAR DIARY or INTELLIGENCE SUMMARY

Army Form C. 2118

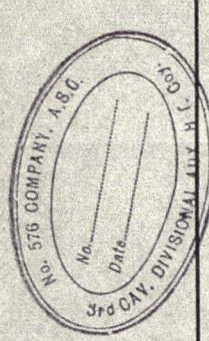

Place	Date	Hour	Summary of Events and Information	Remarks and references to Appendices
BUSNES	18/7/17		Trans: Billets BUSNES. Sgt Grant to "C" Batty to relieve Sgt England. Sgt England to N.S.Y. " " Sgt Grant. Sgt Matthews to Sci. Yeo. " " Sgt Clark. Sgt Collins to 2/9. " " Sgt Curtis.	
do	19/7/17		Trans: Billets as 18/7/17. Sgt Turvin R. " Curtis J. " Clark T. " Curtis R. Leave to U.K. till 29/7 " Slaine J. " Butler C.	
do	20/7/17		Trans: Billets as 18/7/17.	
do	21/7/17		Trans: Billets as 18/7/17.	
do	22/7/17		Trans: Billets as 18/7/17. Inspection of harness received from Base. 6 Reinforcements	
do	23/7/17		Trans: Billets as 18/7/17. Marching order parade & gas drill. 1 R. Horse 2 mules from Base Remounts	
do	24/7/17		Trans: Billets as 18/7/17. Sgt Smith to H.Q. 7 Sgt Graham to relieve St Alban. Sgt Graham 6 men from Base for leave	
do	25/7/17		Trans: Billets as 18/7/17. Parade of Box Wares W.N. Buckley Capt 6 O/c 3 Cav. Div. Div. Amm. H.T. Coy	

WAR DIARY
or
INTELLIGENCE SUMMARY.

Place	Date	Hour	Summary of Events and Information	Remarks and references to Appendices
BUSNES	26/7/17		Troops Billets BUSNES. Sgt. W. Graham, Pte Adams & Pte Atwell H. Sr. Brown G.T. Ritchie R. Gustard R. Hodgson G.H. O'Shaughnessy W. Inman J.W. Scott H. Cpl. Ruddock & horse from 6th Ble. 1 horse from H.Q. 8th Ble. 1 horse changed for Lieut. Neo.	
"	27/7/17		Troops & Billets as 26/7/17. 1 mule changed at 2 L.G. Estb. reduced by 1 horse for Offrs. increased by 1 bicycle. 7/15443 2/Cpl King H. to F.P. 16/7/17. T/035875 Pte Reed J. to H.Q. 23/7/17. 1 Army horse stuck on lines to be taken on strength with ML 2 SS. HQ 3 CD. 2 2017	
"	28/7/17		Troops & Billets as 26/7/17.	
"	29/7/17		Troops & Billets as 26/7/17.	
"	30/7/17		Troops & Billets as 26/7/17. Gas mask & musketry & hot parade. Inman from Regt. for leave.	
"	31/7/17		Troops & Billets as 26/7/17. 3 men from Col. Neo. for leave. Bathing parade.	

W.N. Buckley Capt
O.C. 3 Cav Div. Aux. H.T. Coy.

WAR DIARY or INTELLIGENCE SUMMARY

Army Form C. 2118.

30 Cav D Divn 47 Coy
Vol 19

Place	Date	Hour	Summary of Events and Information	Remarks and references to Appendices
BUSNES	1/8/17		Billets and dump BUSNES Railhead AIRE	
do	2/8/17		B.D.-R. as 1/8/17. 1 Sgt 1 Pet. Sgt 12 D's leave to U.K. till 12/8/17. N°53587 Pte R. Cushing R.F.A. to Base Depot.	
do	3/8/17		B.D.-R. as 1/8/17. nil.	
do	4/8/17		B.D.-R. as 1/8/17.	
do	5/8/17		B.D.-R. as 1/8/17.	
do	6/8/17		B.D.-R. as 1/8/17. 1 mule to 14 M.V.S. 1 Bicycle from O.O. Base. Marching order parade & gas drill.	
do	7/8/17		B.D.-R. as 1/8/17. H/Cpl Latham A. St Brunton J. St Lane W. from Base Depot.	
do	8/8/17		B.D.-R. as 1/8/17.	
do	9/8/17		B.D.-R. as 1/8/17. 2/Lt. T.E.W.D. Simpson St Smith E. leave to U.K. till 19/8/17.	
do	10/8/17		B.D.-R. as 1/8/17.	
do	11/8/17		B.D.-R. as 1/8/17. Pte Neale W. to 2 LG. Pte Partridge E. Pte Cookman to 3 D.G.	
do	12/8/17		B.D.-R. as 1/8/17. St Hill A. St Guille C. St Metcalfe J. R.F.A. elsn II proffer from 14/8/17. 2/5/17 5/6	

W.N. Buckley Capt
Offg 3 Cav Bre Group T Coy

Army Form C. 2118.

WAR DIARY
or
INTELLIGENCE SUMMARY.
(Erase heading not required.)

Instructions regarding War Diaries and Intelligence Summaries are contained in F. S. Regs., Part II. and the Staff Manual respectively. Title pages will be prepared in manuscript.

Place	Date	Hour	Summary of Events and Information	Remarks and references to Appendices
BUSNES	13/8/17		Billets and Stuff BUSNES Railhead AIRE.	
do	14/8/17		B D & R as 13/8/17. 1 Team & 2 Dr from "G" Battery for exchange.	
do	15/8/17		B D & R as 13/8/17	
do	16/8/17		B D & R as 13/8/17. Dr. P. Burns, T. Piron, Dr. Roberts. W. E. Tarpman, Pte. Shuttleworth E. leave to U.K. till 26/8/17	
do	17/8/17		B D & R as 13/8/17. Dr Streatfield W.C. to HB 1 C.D. mule from No 14 V.S.	
do	18/8/17		B D & R as 13/8/17. Dr Stamp T. appd 2/Cpll. 18/7 with fee from 17/7 5/- Far. Sgt Allen W. to 1st Div. Train.	
do	19/8/17		B D & R as 13/8/17. Pte Mullan T.C. to HB	
do	20/8/17		B D & R as 13/8/17.	
do	21/8/17		B D & R as 13/8/17. Dr. Munger Rodger with 1 team of mules from Essex Yeo to G. Bty. Dr. Lowes & Waters to Essex Yeo with 1 team.	
do	22/8/17		B D & R as 13/8/17. Essex. R. Ellis. Dr. Hilliar & Hughes leave to U.K. until 2/9/17	
do	23/8/17		B D & R as 13/8/17	
do	24/8/17		B D & R as 13/8/17	76 N Buckley Capt. dg 3 Cav Bde Aux H.T. Coy

Army Form C. 2118.

WAR DIARY
or
INTELLIGENCE SUMMARY.
(Erase heading not required.)

Place	Date	Hour	Summary of Events and Information	Remarks and references to Appendices
BUSNES	25/8/17		Billets . Dump BUSNES Railhead AIRE 3rd Cav. Bde. Horse Show. Class XIII G.S. wagon mule team won by this Coy.	
do	26/8/17		Sto. Rickets G.S. Chapman N.T. leave to U.K. 27/8/17 till 9/9/17	
do	27/8/17	B.D. R w 25/8/17	L/D. No 236 evacuated to 73 M.V.S.	
do	28/8/17	B.D. R w 25/8/17	L/D. No 17 Med. Cafe M/S Buckley. Cpl Risby. L/Cpl Chiswick St Fost Smith Sto. Bevell, Walker Cavanagh, Mooney, Nawathay & Mannes with 1 G.S. wagon 5 horses and 4 mules proceeded to CROISETTE Medical Inspection & bathing parade	
do	29/8/17	B.D. R w 25/8/17		
do	30/8/17	B.D. R w 25/8/17	L/Cpl Stamp Sr. Allen S.V. Whitehead T. Baxter H. leave to U.K. till 9/9/17	
do	31/8/17	B.D. R w 25/8/17	Sto. Tom, Pte Bishop leave to U.K. till 10/9/17. 1/Cpl Pinckley Cafe to N. Pinckley H. T. Coy.	

Vol 26.

War Diary
for
September, 1917

3rd Cav. Div. Aux. H.T.C.

WAR DIARY or INTELLIGENCE SUMMARY.

Army Form C. 2118.

Instructions regarding War Diaries and Intelligence Summaries are contained in F.S. Regs., Part II. and the Staff Manual respectively. Title pages will be prepared in manuscript.

September 1917.

(Erase heading not required.)

Place	Date	Hour	Summary of Events and Information	Remarks and references to Appendices
BUSNES	1/9/17		Billets BUSNES. Railhead AIRE. 250. Green's English leave to U.K. 1/9/17 to 11/9/17. Cav. Corps Horse Show. G.S. Major's mule team went from Coy.	
"	2/9/17		B & R as 1/9/17. 2nd Lieut. Allen rejoined from Base. H.T.D.	
"	3/9/17		B & R as 1/9/17. 250. Shuwardson H. & Bletcher P.H. from Base H.T.D.	
"	4/9/17		B & R as 1/9/17. 1 L.D. horse evacuated by "K" Batty 24/7.	
"	5/9/17		B & R as 1/9/17. Marching order parade. Pte Cavanagh to Divn Bn. 1 L.D. horse to HQ 6 Cav. Bde. 73/05961 Pte Brown W. to HP.	
"	6/9/17		B & R as 1/9/17. Officers Kendall. S.S. Rugby M.T. & Lieut Buck G. St Knight J. St Beal G. Plot Hunt J. leave to U.K. till 16/9/17. 2 L.D. horses 1 L.D. mule & M720 M.V.S. St Hounstoy to 6 Cav. Bde. St Shenton from 6 Cav Bde to RHQ.	
"	7/9/17		B & R as 1/9/17. St. Brunton G. to 249. St Collins G. from Divn Bn.	
"	8/9/17		B & R as 1/9/17. nil.	
"	9/9/17		B & R as 1/9/17. S.S. Sinclair H. St Hutchings F.W. from Base Dpt C.	
"	10/9/17		B & R as 1/9/17.	

WAR DIARY
or
INTELLIGENCE SUMMARY.

Army Form C. 2118.

Month: September 1917.

Place	Date	Hour	Summary of Events and Information	Remarks and references to Appendices
BUSNES	11/9/17		Billets BUSNES Railhead AIRE. St Tony H.C. from N.S.Y. St Collier & 6th S.J. Marching order parade this will to night	
"	12/9/17		B+R as 11/9/17. Priv. Lyt. Allen W. to S Rest Park.	
"	13/9/17		B+R as 11/9/17. Cpl. Rathbone Paw. Consumpt. 75th Con. F.C. St Tropa - St Tony. Pl. Battre sent to U.K. ett 23/7	
"	14/9/17		B+R as 11/9/17. Tpr. Cpl. Chidwick to H.P. St. Chance W. from Fam Depot.	
"	15/9/17		B+R as 11/9/17. Dr Parry + Fountain & know from "K" Battery. Harness Inspection	
"	16/9/17		B+R as 11/9/17. Lft McDougall M'Derkyshire, Francis Hyger leave to U.K. ett 26/9/17	
			Dr Butcher & Schingell & knew to "K" Battery. Dr Roberts T.W. to hospital.	
"	17/9/17		B+R as 11/9/17 Marching order & Sc drill. Medical Inspection	
"	18/9/17		B+R as 11/9/17 Dr Chapman D.J. to hospital. Dr Renton to 10th Hussars to relieve Horry	
"	19/9/17		B+R as 11/9/17 Dr Knight to 9th Bde. Dr Matthews from 9th Bde.	

E. Danus Kingford 2/Lt
for O.C. 3rd Cav. Div. Amm. H.T.C.

Army Form C. 2118.

WAR DIARY
or
INTELLIGENCE SUMMARY.
(Erase heading not required.)

Instructions regarding War Diaries and Intelligence Summaries are contained in F. S. Regs., Part II. and the Staff Manual respectively. Title pages will be prepared in manuscript.

Place	Date	Hour	Summary of Events and Information	Remarks and references to Appendices
BUSNES	20/9/17	Billets	BUSNES Railhead AIRE. Dr Roberts T.W. from H.	
"	21/9/17	B.H.P. as 20/9/17	Dr Chapman Adj. from H.	
"	22/9/17	B.H.P. as 20/9/17	Harness Inspection. Dr Armstrong & from Base Depot	
"	23/9/17	B.H.P. as 20/9/17	nil	
"	24/9/17	B.H.P. as 20/9/17	M/Cab(?) from H. Pat Method H. D.M. Redman Holt Jones Knox Mungo Gave E.U.K. til 4.10.17	
"	25/9/17	B.H.P. as 20/9/17	2nd anniversary of formation of Company.	
"	26/9/17	B.H.P. as 20/9/17	Inspection by A.D. of V.T. C.C.	
"	27/9/17	B.H.P. as 21/9/17	Rifle Inspection & Gas drill	
"	28/9/17	B.H.P. as 21/9/17	Capt. W.W. Bradley to Duchess of Westminster Hospital.	
"	29/9/17	B.H.P. as 20/9/17	Cpl. Bailey W.S. Collins Lander & Acting Leave E.U.K. til 9.10.17	
"	30/9/17	B.H.P. as 21/9/17	nil.	

E. Dawson Simpson
for O.C. 3rd Div. Aux. H.T. Co.

War Diary of 3rd Cavalry Div. A.M.I.Co

October, 1917

Army Form C. 2118.

WAR DIARY
or
INTELLIGENCE SUMMARY.
(Erase heading not required.)

Instructions regarding War Diaries and Intelligence Summaries are contained in F. S. Regs., Part II. and the Staff Manual respectively. Title pages will be prepared in manuscript.

No. 575 COMPANY, A.S.C.
Date October 1917
3rd CAV. DIVISIONAL AUX. H.T. Coy.

Place	Date	Hour	Summary of Events and Information	Remarks and references to Appendices
BUSNES	1/10/17	Billets	BUSNES Packed AIRE. San. Cpl. Brown from 41st Ord. Train appointed Farrier Sergeant vice San. Sgt. Allen to 8th R.S. Park on appointment to San. Prof Sergeant 11.9.17. Marching Order & Gas Drill	
"	2/10/17	B.&R. as 1/10/17	Pte. Cpl. Clarke from Base Depot. Bakery Parade	
"	3/10/17	B.&R. as 1/10/17	8 Mules from No 4 Base Remount Depot	
"	4/10/17	B.&R. as 1/10/17	nil.	
"	5/10/17	B.&R. as 1/10/17	nil	
"	6/10/17	B.&R. as 1/10/17	S.S. Bayley & A.S.C. Base Depot 2 L.D. horses from 3rd Spare Squadron (to be shown in command)	
"	7/10/17	B.&R. as 1/10/17	10 Tommes S. from Base Depot	
"	8/10/17	B.&R. as 1/10/17	All Transport attached to Units returned to H.Q. except "C" & "S" Batteries R.H.A. 37 wagons 148 animals 72 personnel	E.N.P

Army Form C. 2118.

WAR DIARY
or
INTELLIGENCE SUMMARY.
(Erase heading not required.)

Instructions regarding War Diaries and Intelligence Summaries are contained in F. S. Regs., Part II. and the Staff Manual respectively. Title pages will be prepared in manuscript.

Place	Date	Hour	Summary of Events and Information	Remarks and references to Appendices
BUSNES	9/10/17		Billets BUSNES Railhead AIRE 1 L.D. & 81 Coy A.S.C.	
"	10/10/17		BHR as 9/10/17 Establishment of Company increased by 2 Riddles (incl 1 Corporal) Auth: Adv. f.102. G.S. O.R.S. /1998 7/10/17	
"	11/10/17		BHR as 9/10/17 Changed team Mules for horses with 6th Bde. H.Q.	
"	12/10/17		BHR as 9/10/17 1 mule evacuated to "G" Batt. R.H.A. 6/9/17	
"	13/10/17		BHR as 9/10/17 nil.	
"	14/10/17		BHR as 9/10/17 nil.	
"	15/10/17		BHR as 9/10/17 nil.	
"	16/10/17		BHR as 9/10/17 All transport sent out to Regiments to complete 13 wagons per Brigade. 37 wagons 149 animals 73 personnel	
"	17/10/17		Company moved from BUSNES to PERNES.	

E.D.S.

Army Form C. 2118.

WAR DIARY
or
INTELLIGENCE SUMMARY.

(Erase heading not required.)

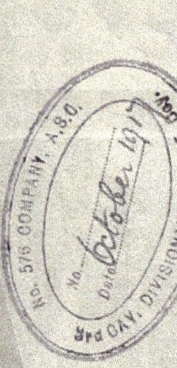
No. 5/6 COMPANY. A.S.C.
Date October 1917
3rd CAV. DIVISIONAL AUX. H.T. COY.

Place	Date	Hour	Summary of Events and Information	Remarks and references to Appendices
PERNES	18/10/17		Billets PERNES. Railhead AIRE. Dr. Chaver 14 days F.P.N.º 2 + forfeits 2 days pay G.R.W.	
"	19/10/17		B.A.R. as 19/10/17 Nil.	
"	20/10/17		B.A.R. as 19/10/17 Capt. W.N. Buckley from Hospital	
"	21/10/17		B.A.R. as 19/10/17 1 mule evacuated to Essex Fm. 21/9/17 Replaced by 1 mule	
"	22/10/17		B.A.R. as 19/10/17 nil	
"	23/10/17		Company moved from PERNES to HOUVIN-HOUVIGNEUL	
HOUVIN	23/10/17		Company moved to DOMART. Capt. W.N. BUCKLEY Leave to U.K. until 2/11/17	
DOMART	24/10/17		Billets DOMART. Railhead CANDAS	
"	25/10/17		B.A.R. as 24/10/17 Nil.	

G.D.V.

WAR DIARY
or
INTELLIGENCE SUMMARY.

Army Form C. 2118.

Place	Date	Hour	Summary of Events and Information	Remarks and references to Appendices
DOMART.	26/10/17		B.V.R. as 24/10/17. Div. Tank wagon & 1 team horses & harness to Rett	
"	27/10/17		do. Dr. Baxter transferred to Royal Irish.	
"	28/10/17		d. 1 L.D. to N° M.V.S. 1 " destroyed at 10th Hussars.	
"	29/10/17		d. Dr. Ed. Palmer W.C. Dr. Baine N. Dr. Stinson A. from Base Depot	
"	30/10/17		d. 1 G.S. Wagon from 10th Hussars for repairs. 1 L.D. to 10 Hussars to complete.	
"	31/10/17		d. 1 L.D. evacuated by 8th M.B.S.	

E. Dawes Simpson
Capt.
a/y 3rd Cav. Div. Amc. Horse Transport O.

Vol ≠ 22

War Diary of
3 Cavalry Div. Hqrs. A.I.F.
for November 1917

WAR DIARY or INTELLIGENCE SUMMARY

Army Form C. 2118.

No. 576 COMPANY, A.S.C.
3rd CAV. DIVISIONAL AUX. H.T. Coy.

Place	Date	Hour	Summary of Events and Information	Remarks and references to Appendices
DOMART	1/4/17		Billets DOMART Railhead CANDOS 2 L.D. horses from Am. Col.	
"	2/4/17		do	
"	3/4/17		do	Nil.
"	4/4/17		do	1 mule to N.S. Yeo. 1 horse to Fld. Sqd.
"	5/4/17		do	Sgt. McTavish AVC and SS Bennett and Tomkins to Divisional School DAO.R.S.
"	6/4/17		do	T/4/041176 Dr. Boyd.R. 14 days OC. Baths, strenuous return. Parade gas drill.
"	7/4/17		do	4 mules changed with Gro S.T. Barrage for 4 horses
"	8/4/17		do	Routine. Increased establishment of 2 muledrawn pr. col. W.O. letter 121/France/1220 (SD 2) dt. 2.11.17
"	9/4/17		do	Routine. 067876 Lce Cpl. Lidholm T.S. 3692 SS Walbert. T.2863.27 dt Scott W.O. leave to UK till 22.11.17
"	10/4/17		do	Routine. T.239122 SS Tomkins H. to G.2 Sub Coy to pay 10/9/17 Routine Ygr. Dr Elliot A. T6902 Dr. Mundin WJ. leave UK till 24/11/17 Gas drill

WAR DIARY or INTELLIGENCE SUMMARY

Army Form C. 2118.

Place	Date	Hour	Summary of Events and Information	Remarks and references to Appendices
DOMART	11/11/17		40Us DOMART-Maulined CAMPAS. Route: Innuels to evacuated to 13 M V S by 1st RD 1 LD evacuated to 20 M V S by 5th M.G.S. T/4 067297 "La Brecke" Boyce R. J. afternoon T/4 057876 " " Selleton W.J. Geo Gibs T/4 057220 " " Stamp T T/4 058676 "Cpl. Kelly W.S. promoted corporal 	
"	12/11/17		do Marching order parade T/4 144219 D. Shuman F. granted 1st S.B. days 25/10/17 T/4 144785 " Linakie R " " 6/11/17 T/4 144789 " Linaker W " " 6/11/17 T/1/8 " Simms T " " 29/10/17 RTA 20409 " Whitehead " " 29/10/17 T/4 058160 Dr. Harris L.a. 14 days F.P. No 2 120 evacuated by 1st gr. B.C. at War. 	
"	13/11/17		do Capt. W. Buckley to Hospital on England 2/11/17 T/4 044822 Cpl. Bathune A.E. to Hospital	

WAR DIARY
INTELLIGENCE SUMMARY

Army Form C. 2118.

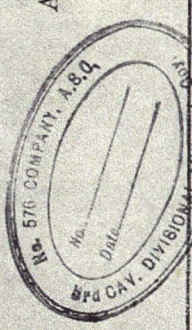

Place	Date	Hour	Summary of Events and Information	Remarks and references to Appendices
DOMART	14/11/17		Billets DOMART. Railhead CANDAS. Routine I.C.D to H.Q. 6th hour spent to replace wagon returned X.R.H. Sergt Hughes continued once weekly children's school. Recd 1916 (January) 4/11/17	
"	15/11/17		J.O.R. from A.S.C train depot. 1 mule to S.O.G.S to replace animal wound. Farrier, chemical instruction (Gas in)	
"	16/11/17		Routine. 1/2 087,067 T. Lewis 28 hospital mule-evacuation. 4 1st R.D.	
"	17/11/17		Routine	
"	18/11/17		Company moved DOMART to ETINEHEM, Railhead LA FLAQUE	
ETINEHEM	19/11/17		Billets ETINEHEM, Railhead LA FLAQUE. Transport returned from Heilly with exception of Steam? & wagon, 2 L.G. carolier ammunition from Amm Park 27 rounds 18 pr & 28 rds 6 A.A. 2500 flares & R H.A. Gunners from Amm Park 1.99? 3 gunners & horses from 6/3 Dragoons. Col. Lafs, Major West from field hoist. Capt Bartrue took over Company. " Phipps in and return to 18 HHS.	
"	20/11/17		do	
"	21/11/17		do. 2 riding horses & 3rd class gun team to S dep H. 14 036/85 Pt. Blackmack 28 days F.P. No1 1 Pte one days pay	EWS

WAR DIARY
INTELLIGENCE SUMMARY

Army Form C. 2118

Place	Date	Hour	Summary of Events and Information	Remarks and references to Appendices
ETINEHEM	22/4/17		Billets ETINEHEM. Received Ammunition, accepted at ETINEHEM myron N.T. 16 nynomito + nynoreno No 5. Gr Kot Rot 4 mudo nynomito + nynoreno No 5. Gr Kot Rot 4 mudo from Base	
	23/4/17		Company moved to BEAUQUESNE. 4 Gunner R Hazelwood to Ammn Park 1 Cpl 3 Gunners to Ammn Col.	
BEAUQUESNE	24/4/17		15 With BEAUQUESNE Nothing BELLE EGLISE Routine	
"	25/4/17		do do Routine Gas drill	
"	26/4/17		do Do Tc3464 Dr Sac Effray N4 from 4 "Rio Fast & applies army Sad GNE 5/10/17. 1 mule passing twen to 20 N/5 chatchy adon parade, Gas drill 10 R-G Hospital	
"	27/4/17		do Do T/2 03/28 Dr Lane M 25 days F.P.No 2 TRD 1812 Lane # + 1. " 3.O.R.4 drawn to Divisional School	
"	28/4/17		do do Routine	
"	29/4/17		do do Routine	
"	30/4/17		Company moved from BEAUQUESNE to CORBIE	

E.W. Bates. Capt
OC 576 Coy Div Aux Horse Transpt

Army Form C. 2118.

WAR DIARY
or
INTELLIGENCE SUMMARY.
(Erase heading not required.)

H.T. Coy
December 1917

3 Coy D Aux VA2

Place	Date	Hour	Summary of Events and Information	Remarks and references to Appendices
CORBIE	1/12/17		Billets CORBIE. Rashino BELLE EGLISE Routine + embarkation tone commands	
"	2/12/17		do	Routine, 1 mule destroyed 2 L.G.
"	3/12/17		do	Horses billets at CORBIE
"	4/12/17		do	Routine
"	5/12/17		do	Routine, Tank report to 7. M.S.S. standing
"				new horses
"	6/12/17		do	Routine
"	7/12/17		do	CORBIE Routine
"	8/12/17		do	Routine
"	9/12/17		do	CORBIE Routine
"				St. Matthews from Divsupply pk tkt
"				1 mule evacuated to 48 Mob. V.S. Nouvion
"	10/12/17		do	Routine Tk 470 St S. Thompson returned Sgt 139/017
"				Tk 47996 Lo Cpl. Latham W/jenkins 2668977
"	11/12/17		do	Routine 1.L.D. to Lincoln Gro.
"	12/12/17		do	Routine 7296/77 Pte Renton R to have report
"	13/12/17		do	Routine 1 mule anchored 1 Pte Rosegren
"	14/12/17		do	Routine 1 mule to 7th 88th xplace

Army Form C. 2118.

December 1917

WAR DIARY
or
INTELLIGENCE SUMMARY.
(Erase heading not required.)

Instructions regarding War Diaries and Intelligence Summaries are contained in F. S. Regs., Part II. and the Staff Manual respectively. Title pages will be prepared in manuscript.

Place	Date	Hour	Summary of Events and Information	Remarks and references to Appendices
CORBIE	16/12/17		Attd. CORBIE Haulriad CORBIE. Routine. 2nd Lt Mc Dougall exchange with Pay M/Lt Good. Enlist 2 sgt N.C.O Depot 21/12/17	
"	16/12/17		do. Nothing of 2/17 2nd Lt 2 N R Williamson to fund there	
"	17/12/17		do. Routine	
"	18/12/17		do. do	
"	19/12/17		do. do	
"	20/12/17		do. do 2/Lt EuD turf/mp hospital	
"	21/12/17		Company moved from CORBIE to DOMART EN PONTHIEU 120	
DOMART	22/12/17		Total. DOMART Haulriad CANDAS. Routine	
"	23/12/17		do. do	
"	24/12/17		do. Routine 2 mules from here removed dept	
"	25/12/17		do. Routine	
"	26/12/17		do. Routine. Nation for the purpose of as from withdrawn	
"	27/12/17		do. Routine T16959 Cpl Murray T.B.H.S.S. Rusley to Kendale H/S 4th Q.27 rank Cavs.	
"	28/12/17		do. Routine 5th Army 5th army ordam nghl as 32:50	
"	29/12/17		do. Army Authy for dgchy southeby discharged 8 oct 33	
			Routine	

GWB

Army Form C. 2118.

3 December 1917

WAR DIARY
or
INTELLIGENCE SUMMARY.
(Erase heading not required.)

Place	Date	Hour	Summary of Events and Information	Remarks and references to Appendices
DOMART-Northern CANDAS	30/12/17		Forlish DOMART-Northern CANDAS Dowkins taken duty. T/037832 Lt Sparrow W T/21676 Lt Day H T/225 Lt Troyeth S.S.C. T/167716 " Foster P Jones Moss Septh HARE Newhire and ration duty.	
"	31/12/17		do	

E.W. Sadler Capt.
O.C. 3rd Cav. Div. Auxiliary Horse Transport Co.

Army Form C. 2118.

WAR DIARY
or
INTELLIGENCE SUMMARY.
(Erase heading not required.)

Instructions regarding War Diaries and Intelligence Summaries are contained in F. S. Regs., Part II. and the Staff Manual respectively. Title pages will be prepared in manuscript.

11 T Coyf
Vol 24

Place	Date	Hour	Summary of Events and Information	Remarks and references to Appendices
Field	Jan 1 1918		Billets DOMART Routhéac CANDAS Routine	
	2		"	
	3		"	
	4		"	19 mules unserviceable, to remounts
	5-8		"	
	9		"	Horse casualty framed by DR. 1 for LD Cont
	10-13		"	2 L Donaiste and 99 R
	14-17		"	
	18		Company moved DOMART to ST LEGER-LES-DOMART	
	19		Billets ST LEGER LES DOMART Routhéac CANDAS – Routine 2/Lt E.D.Simpson returned to Company from B4TD
	20		"	Lieut Nahmi & HT pro 6 Car Wold
	21-25		"	Lieut and 21 reinforcements for 6 Car fale
	26-28		"	Routine

Army Form C. 2118.

WAR DIARY
or
INTELLIGENCE SUMMARY

(Erase heading not required.)

Instructions regarding War Diaries and Intelligence Summaries are contained in F. S. Regs., Part II. and the Staff Manual respectively. Title pages will be prepared in manuscript.

Place	Date	Hour	Summary of Events and Information	Remarks and references to Appendices
Field	29		Company moved to PROYART a long journey of 86 kilometres taking 9 a.m. and arriving at 9.30 p.m.	
"	30			
"	31		Company moved from PROYART to ESTRÉES-EN-CHAUSSÉE Billets ESTRÉES-EN-CHAUSSÉE Nature	

E.W. Butler Capt.
O.C. 5 Res. Ser. A.H.T. 30

Army Form C. 2118.

WAR DIARY
or
~~INTELLIGENCE SUMMARY~~
(Erase heading not required.)

Instructions regarding War Diaries and Intelligence Summaries are contained in F. S. Regs., Part II. and the Staff Manual respectively. Title pages will be prepared in manuscript.

Apx H/Coy
3 Coy D
Vol 25

Place	Date	Hour	Summary of Events and Information	Remarks and references to Appendices
Field	1918 Feb 1		Billets ESTRÉES-EN-CHAUSSÉE Routine	
"	2-6		" "	
"	7		" " Horse respirators issued	
"	8-24		" "	
"	25		Railhead MONS-EN-CHAUSSÉE "	
"	26-28		" "	

E W Wakeslake
OC 3rd Bar Sec AHTD.

Army Form C. 2118.

WAR DIARY
or ~~INTELLIGENCE SUMMARY~~

March 1918

(Erase heading not required.)

Instructions regarding War Diaries and Intelligence Summaries are contained in F. S. Regs., Part II. and the Staff Manual respectively. Title pages will be prepared in manuscript.

Place	Date	Hour	Summary of Events and Information	Remarks and references to Appendices
Field	1/3/15		Billets ESTRÉES EN CHAUSSÉE Railroad MONS Routine, returns dealt with. Low transport for Railroad	
	2/3/15		"	
	3/3/15		"	4 LD from base
	4/3/15 – 5/3/15		"	Routine. Remount 8 4OZ
	9/3/15		"	Routine. Tournament
	10–12/3/15		"	" commenced 11 A.m. 9/3/15
	13/3/15		Company moved to MONS EN CHAUSSÉE	"
	14–19/3/15		Billets MONS EN CHAUSSÉE Railhead BRIE Routine	
	20/3/15		"	10 wagons 2 GDR and
	21/3/15		"	4 OLD wagons from 5th Reg.t Rec.
	21/3/15		"	9 wagons and teams to Canadian Carpse
	22/3/15		"	H.Q.rs 11 wagons & teams to Canadian Carpse
	22/3/15		Company moved MONS EN CHAUSSÉE to VARESNES	transport
			VARESNES to CARLEPONT	1 mule LD wounded & cast
	23/3/15		"	
	24/3/15		Billets CARLEPONT. Routine. 1 wounded mule evacuated	

Army Form C. 2118.

WAR DIARY
or
INTELLIGENCE SUMMARY.
(Erase heading not required.)

Instructions regarding War Diaries and Intelligence
Summaries are contained in F. S. Regs., Part II.
and the Staff Manual respectively. Title pages
will be prepared in manuscript.

No. 576 COMPANY, A.S.C.
3rd CAV. DIVISIONAL AUX. M.T. COY.

March 1918

Place	Date	Hour	Summary of Events and Information	Remarks and references to Appendices
Field	25/3/18		Company marched from CARLEPONT to TRACY-LE-MONT	
	26/3/18		Company marched TRACY-LE-MONT to COMPIEGNE	
	27/3/18		Billets COMPIEGNE Routine	
	28/3/18		" "	
	29/3/18		Company moved from COMPIEGNE to LES GARICHOUS, AVRECHY	
	30/3/18		Company moved from LES GARICHOUS, AVRECHY to WALLY	
	31/3/18		Billets WALLY Routine	

E.W. Salby, Captain
O.C. 3rd Cav. Div. Aux. M.T. Co.

Army Form C. 2118.

WAR DIARY
or
INTELLIGENCE SUMMARY

(Erase heading not required.)

Instructions regarding War Diaries and Intelligence Summaries are contained in F. S. Regs., Part II. and the Staff Manual respectively. Title pages will be prepared in manuscript.

Vol 27

No. _____ Date April 19_ _
No. 576 COMPANY, A.S.C.
3rd CAV. DIVISIONAL AUX. H.T.

Place	Date	Hour	Summary of Events and Information	Remarks and references to Appendices
Field	1918 April 1		Company moved from WAILLY to PONT DE METZ. 2 L.D. horses marched. Remainder by trains	
	" 2		Billets PONT DE METZ Railhead AMIENS. Routine	
	" 3-5		"	
	" 6		Company moved to RIVERY. L.D. horses evacuated by Canadian Van 1960	
	" 7-10		Billets RIVERY Railhead AMIENS Routine	
	" 11		Company moved to LONG	
	" 12		Billets LONG. Four tank wagons with drivers and teams complete to Carbapho Reinforcement Camp for duty.	
	" 13		Company moved to VAULX.	
	" 14		Billets VAULX Railhead HESDIN Routine	
	" 15		"	
	" 16		"	
	" 17		" — Eight L.D. mules from Remount Camp ABBEVILLE	
	" 18-19		"	

Army Form C. 2118.

WAR DIARY
or
~~INTELLIGENCE SUMMARY~~

(Erase heading not required.)

Instructions regarding War Diaries and Intelligence Summaries are contained in F. S. Regs., Part II. and the Staff Manual respectively. Title pages will be prepared in manuscript.

Place	Date	Hour	Summary of Events and Information	Remarks and references to Appendices
Field	1918 April 20		Bellilo VAULX Maulhuac HESDIN Routine	
			T4/058676 Cpl RIDLEY W.S promoted a/sgt	
			T4/197976 G/2oCpl LATHAM.A a/Cpl	
			T4/058504 Dr BUDD.G a/2ndCpl	
	21-24		Bellilo VAULX Maulhuac HESDIN Routine	
	25-30		AUXI LE CHATEAU Routine, Routine, Routine	
			Moved by own transport	

EWBakes Cap ASC
OC 3rd Cav Div AHT&S

Army Form C. 2118.

Vol 2

Instructions regarding War Diaries and Intelligence Summaries are contained in F. S. Regs., Part II. and the Staff Manual respectively. Title pages will be prepared in manuscript.

WAR DIARY
or
INTELLIGENCE SUMMARY.
(Erase heading not required.)

Place	Date	Hour	Summary of Events and Information	Remarks and references to Appendices
Field	May 1-5		Billets VAUX Nauthier AUX LE CHATEAU Nauleau	
	6		H'd Q'rs of Company moved VAUX to BEALCOURT	
	7		3rd Coy of Company moved from BEALCOURT to SURCAMPS	
	8-16		Billets SURCAMPS Nauthier STLEGER LES DOMART Routine Rations drawn by motor transport from railhead	
	17		3rd Coy of Company moved to BETHENCOURT ST OUEN. New wagons drawn and horses returned from 6" Cav H.Q.	
	18		Billets BETHENCOURT ST OUEN Nauthier ST LEGER LES DOMART. Ten wagons drawn and harness drawn from 7" Cav H.Q. Routine	
	19		"	Rations drawn from railhead
	20.23		"	"
	24		"	"
	25		"	6 horses and 3 lorries at VAL DE MAISON to III Army group rations drawn from railhead for Canadians Cav Bde in
	26-31		"	place of 7" Cav Bde. Eight wagons drawn and horses from 7" Cav Bde Routine Rations drawn from railhead for Canadians Cav Bde

W Salter Capt AVC
O.C. 6.65" Cav Fd AAT U5

Army Form C. 2118.

WAR DIARY
~~INTELLIGENCE~~ SUMMARY.
(Erase heading not required.)

Vol 29

Instructions regarding War Diaries and Intelligence Summaries are contained in F. S. Regs., Part II. and the Staff Manual respectively. Title pages will be prepared in manuscript.

Place	Date	Hour	Summary of Events and Information	Remarks and references to Appendices
Field	June 1918 1		Camp BETTENCOURT, ST OUEN Masthead ST LEGER, LES DOMART troops tent of company 3065ᵃ	
"	2-4		" Cavalry Division	
"	2-14		" Routine	
"	15		" Inspection of Company by 3065ᵃ Cavalry Division	
"	16-18		" Routine	
"	19		" Company inspected by O.C. ALC	
"	20-23		" "	
"	24		" Company inspected by 66.G.O.C	
"	25-30		" "	

Ellerby Capt AC
66 3ᵃ Cav Div AUT.Co.

WAR DIARY

Army Form C. 2118.

INTELLIGENCE SUMMARY
(Erase heading not required.)

Place	Date	Hour	Summary of Events and Information	Remarks and references to Appendices
Field	July 1		Camp BETHENCOURT-ST-OUEN Roulheas ST LEGER-LES-DOMART Divisr HORN totally	Vol 30
"	2-4		Camp " " " Gaylgue " Roulins Games at 7th Cav Bde A.P.S. Routine	
"	5		" Routine. 6 L.G. wagons with teams complete and 1st a carpenter	
"	6-18		" " for H.Q. 3rd Fld Squadron for detachment movement	
"	19		" " Routine	
"	20		" " 4 L.G. wagons with teams to 1st Hqrs R.H.A. for duty	
"	21		" " 6 " " " 6 " "	
"	22		" HAMBEST Routine " 6 Car mob. for duty	
"	23		" " "	
"	24-29		" " "	
"	30		" " (Three water tanks exchanged for L.G. wagons at AH TO ABBEVILLE	
"	31		" " 6 wagons and teams with N 6 schemes pres duty with 3rd Fld Squadron	

Lt Halsey Capt.

WAR DIARY
INTELLIGENCE SUMMARY

Army Form C. 2118.

Place	Date 1918	Hour	Summary of Events and Information	Remarks and references to Appendices
Field	Aug 1-3		156th B BETHENCOURT, Nachrichten HANGEST Brichre	
	4		"	
	5		" Ammunition delivered by M.T. for	
	6		" Encraid out to magno	
	7		Nature Company Hd. BETHENCOURT Billetd PONT DE METZ.	
	8		9.45 am orad prepared as nature of 3rd Can Sui. Army at 6 PONT DE METZ. Company moved in van of 3rd Can Div transpt at 2 am and encamped in fields near Hill 5 k.m. in environs at DOMART SUR LA LUCE. Sgt RIDLEY was wounded at HANGARD by accidental explosion of enemy trench mine to billets at IGNAUCOURT Camp burned at night below casualties	
	9			
	10		Company moved to CAIX and thence to environs WK. WAR VILLERS. Sermo. He was wounded by enemy bomb	
	11		Company moved to REMIEMCOURT.	
	12-14		Billets thence REMIEMCOURT.	
	15		Company moved to BETHENCOURT ST OUEN	

Army Form C. 2118.

WAR DIARY
or
INTELLIGENCE SUMMARY.
(Erase heading not required.)

Instructions regarding War Diaries and Intelligence Summaries are contained in F. S. Regs., Part II. and the Staff Manual respectively. Title pages will be prepared in manuscript.

Place	Date	Hour	Summary of Events and Information	Remarks and references to Appendices
Field	Aug 16		Active BETHENCOURT ST. OUEN Railway	
"	17		" " "	
"	18		Communication handed over to H.A.T.C.	
"	19		" " "	
"	20-24		Railhead HAMELEST Railway	
"	25		" " "	
"	26		En chang moved to CAUMONT	
"	"		" " WILLENCOURT	
"	27-31		Active WILLENCOURT Railhead AUXI LE CHATEAU Railway	

Ed Bates Capt ASC
O.C. 3rd Car. Div: A.H.T.Co.

Stamp: No. 5/6 COMPANY, A.S.C. 3rd CAV. DIVISIONAL AUX.

Army Form C. 2118.

No. 1
September 1918

WAR DIARY
or
INTELLIGENCE SUMMARY

3rd Cavalry Divisional Auxiliary Horse Transport Company

Army Form C. 2118. (Erase heading not required.)

Loss 11. — WILLENCOURT

Place	Date	Hour	Summary of Events and Information	Remarks and references to Appendices
WILLENCOURT	1/9/18		Company at WILLENCOURT. Railhead AUXI-LE-CHATEAU. Strength of Company – Wanting to complete 3 Drivers & 1 L.D. Horse. 1 man to Hospital.	nil
	2/9/18		3 men proceeded on Leave to U.K. 3/9/18 to 17/9/15	nil
	3/9/18		Capt. Willmott M.C. R.A.S.C. attached for Medical Duties with 1 Horse (riding) & 1 Servant	nil
	4/9/18		1 man granted Leave to U.K. 5/9/18 to 19/9/15 – (2 men & 1 Horse riding) W&O Personnel transferred to 3rd Cav. Reserve Park.	nil
	5/9/18		Capt. E.H. Baker handed over command to Lieut. T.S.W.D. Thompson & reported to 37th Divisional Train taking two Horses (riding)	nil
	6/9/15		3 men granted Leave to U.K. 7/9/15 – 21/9/15 – The following punishments were made T/34106 Driver Ruskin J.W. forfeits 15 days pay – T/4,084416 Baker F. forfeits 21 days pay T/2,086661 Dr Savery A. forfeits 10 days pay T/4. 23 A. of Musings of L. 6 months I.L.H.	nil

Army Form C. 2118.

WAR DIARY
or
INTELLIGENCE SUMMARY.
(Erase heading not required.)

3rd Cavalry Divisional
Auxiliary Horse Transport Company
September 1918

Place	Date	Hour	Summary of Events and Information	Remarks and references to Appendices
Lens 11				
MILLENCOURT	2/9/18		1 O.R. rejoined from Base H.T. Dept. 1 G.S. Wagon drawn from DADOS.	m/s
"	5/9/18		Personnel – 7/32955 Dr. Kirby E. awarded 14 days FP N°1. – 4 complete turnouts sent for duty to H.Q. 7th Cavt Bde. – 1 O.R. proceeded to 37th Stat. Train. – 1 O.R. returned to duty from 37th Stat. Train rejoined for duty. Capt. W.E. RIDER	m/s
"	9/9/18		Capt W.E. RIDER took over command of Company. – 6 complete turnout sent for duty to H.Q. 9th Canadian Brigade. – Sjt. 1. Kirby returned from B.H.T.D.	m/s
"	10/9/18		Railhead – FREVENT – 2 Wagons to Railhead. – 2 men proceeded leave to U.K. 11/9/18 to 25/9/18. – W.O./L 4258 D.r. Munge A. struck by Charger.	m/s
"	11/9/18		2 Wagons returned Railhead. – 1 Mule renumerated – 1 I.S. to Hospital. – 1 Horse (charger) from 37th Stat. Train received. – 4 complete turnouts returned from 7th Cav. Bde.	m/s
"	12/9/18		Routine as usual. – Horses taken off Iron & feeding shelters owing to bad condition of horselines.	m/s

3

Army Form C. 2118.

3rd Cavalry Divisional
Auxiliary Horse Transport Company
September 1915

WAR DIARY
or
INTELLIGENCE SUMMARY
(Erase heading not required.)

Place	Date	Hour	Summary of Events and Information	Remarks and references to Appendices
LENS 11				
WILLENCOURT	13/9/15		2 Majors to Southend, return. 1 O.R. to U.K. leave 13/9/15 to 27/9/15 – Conducting Party by D.D.R. 1 L.D. cont. – CSM Hughes to Hospital	
	14/9/15		5 men granted leave to U.K. 15/9/15 to 29/9/15.	
	15/9/15		Company Parade by Vet. O. – CSM Hughes returned from Hospital	
	16/9/15		1 O.R. referred to B.H.T.D. for Medical Board. – 1 Rider 4 L.D. & 1 Mule evacuated to 10th M.V.S. – 1 reinforcement O.R. from B.H.T.D.	
	17/9/15		1 O.R. to 7th C.F.A. for gunnery Medical Dope. Company moved from WILLENCOURT to CHERIENNE	
CHERIENNE	18/9/15		Returns drawn from M.T. Company at VACQUERIE – (2 Wagons) 5 men granted leave to U.K. 18/9/15 to 3/10/15. – Capt. Weldrich M.O. – 1 Servant & 1 Horse to 3rd Line Reserve Park	

WAR DIARY or INTELLIGENCE SUMMARY

Army Form C. 2118.

3rd Cavalry Divisional Auxiliary Horse Transport Company
September 1918

Place	Date	Hour	Summary of Events and Information	Remarks and references to Appendices
LENS II				
CHERIENNE	19/9/18		17 Waggons conveyed Hay from Company to VACQUERIE-LE-BOURG. – Refors drawn from Dumps at CHERIENNE	say
	20/9/18		2 Complete Turnouts detached to "C" Battery R.H.A. 4 complete turnouts detached to 16th R. Hussars. – Routine as usual – 1. O.R. reinforcement from B.H.T.D.	say
	21/9/18		2 O.R. reinforcements from B.H.T.D. – 1 O.R. reported from A.P.M. after serving sentence [Inspection of Company mounted on Marching Order by O.C. – Mont Hose Lines	say
	22/9/18		1 L.D. Horse evacuated to 14th Mobile V.S. 4 complete Turnouts returned from 16th R. Hussars and 2 complete Turnouts from "C" Batty R.H.A.	say
	23/9/18		Say Waggons returned to 1 Base Depot – surplus to Establishment – Routine as usual	say
	24/9/18		1 Waggon exchanged 6th Cav Bde ammunition systems – 2 Grooms 4 L.D. Horses and harness complete handed over on loan to 3rd Brigad Squadron ambulance G.O.C. – 1 O.R. returned leave U.K. – all preparations gassed at gas school –	say
	25/9/18		Company moved from CHERIENNE to AUTHIEULE. – 5 Armstrong Hutts and 56 tents taken over from DAHQ. & carried on transport	say
	26/9/18		Company moved from AUTHIEULE to ALBERT area. 30 Inft handed over	say

Sept. 1918 5

WAR DIARY
or
INTELLIGENCE SUMMARY.

3rd Cavalry Divisional Auxiliary Horse Transport Company Army Form C. 2118.

(Erase heading not required.)

Instructions regarding War Diaries and Intelligence Summaries are contained in F. S. Regs., Part II. and the Staff Manual respectively. Title pages will be prepared in manuscript.

Place	Date	Hour	Summary of Events and Information	Remarks and references to Appendices
LENS. 11. ALBERT Sheet 12. c. H.S.C cond.	27/9/18		Company moved from ALBERT to H.S.C. cornfield (Sheet 62.c.) Slipviel Routine	
	28/9/18			
	29/9/18		1 complete turnout returned from each of 6th, 7th & Canadian Brigades & attached (1 shed of Headquarter tub-section to 3rd Can-Div Reserve Park). 1 shed of Headquarter tub-section to 3rd Can-Div Reserve Park. Light Section. - 1 Help sent to Ordnance. Company attached to Cavalry Corps Troops. - 1 O.R. sent to Can: Canteen	
	30/9/18		Slipviel Routine As the date - Strength of Company. 2 Officers rank deplaced 3 riding horses surplus 3 L.D. (non) deficient. Health of Company good & condition of horses transport fair. No battle casualties during month.	

W.J. Miles Sgt.
O.C. 3rd Can Div. A.H.T.

WJM

Army Form C. 2118.

3rd Cavalry Divisional
Auxiliary Horse Transport Company
57th Company ASC

WAR DIARY
or
INTELLIGENCE SUMMARY.
(Erase heading not required.)

Instructions regarding War Diaries and Intelligence Summaries are contained in F. S. Regs., Part II. and the Staff Manual respectively. Title pages will be prepared in manuscript.

Army Form C. 2118.

Place	Date	Hour	Summary of Events and Information	Remarks and references to Appendices
Sheet 62.C H.S.C. coupré	1/10/15		Company detailed as ordered - Railhead H.5.B.2.2 (Sheet 62 C) Strength of Company 3 Horses (riding) overstrength. 3 Horses L.D. understrength. 2 other ranks understrength.	
	2/10/15		Company now attached to 3rd Echelon Cavalry Corps - routine as usual	
	3/10/15		Company inspected on Field Marshal's orders (Reinforcement) by O.C.	
	4/10/15		2 Wagons preferred Railhead - 2 Wagon loads of Stores collected ex Railhead - 1 O.R. from time routine as usual	
	5/10/15		3 O.R. returned leave U.K. O.C. inspected all detached transport units 6/7th & Canadian Brigades. Some attached to normal at midnight.	
	6/10/15		2 O.R. returned from leave U.K. But particular parade. Routine as usual	
	7/10/15		5 O.R. returned leave U.K. routine as usual	
	8/10/15		T/037772 Dr. Wilkinson D. struck off strength from 12/8/15 - 1 Riding Horse evacuated 13th V.E.S.	
	9/10/15		T/26755 Driver Day H. and T/3275 Dr. Pretley B. despatched to ASC Base depot for transfer to 3rd Y.E.S. 16 Infantry - 1 L.D. Horse evacuated to 3rd K.21.C.	
Sheet 62 C. K.21.C coupré	10/10/15		Company moved to K. 21. C. coupré (Sheet 62 C) 10 miles 29050 Cpl. Redcliffe - RFA attached arranged for E.Pro. 2. - M.T. 370222 Dr. Stevenson J.W. to hospital	
	11/10/15			

High Reference

3rd County (unnamed?)
Sheet 62.O.
K.21.C. central
Auxiliary Horse Transport Company

WAR DIARY
or
INTELLIGENCE SUMMARY.
(Erase heading not required.)

Army Form C. 2118.

Place	Date	Hour	Summary of Events and Information	Remarks and references to Appendices
Sheet 62.C. K.21.C. central	12/10/15		Reached TINCOURT - D.Sheet.5. 77,560 guarded General Store to U.K. Y/10/15,5,23/10,15	say
	13/10/15		14 grooms detailed to convey papers for "B" Echelon from railhead to camp - railhead	say
			ROISEL STATION.	
	14/10/15		Company moved to U.10.B.2.5. (Sheet 57 C) 15 miles	say
	15/10/15		Roulgné as usual. O.C. A.S.C. inspected Horse Troops - 6 L.D.Trucks fallen in strength	say
			1 Company from Hqr Gun Car Btte	
Up.B.2.5.	16/10/15		Routine as usual - Main road - ROCQUIGNY - 3 Kilometres	say
	17/10/15		do Marching Order prepared by O.C.	say
	18/10/15		Board of Enquiry held on Ty/239,122 S.S. Smithers H. to not reported on his efficiency as a cold officer - Finding - dispersed - 6 L.D. (black) & 9 L.L.D. inside (same) decreased to 13 M.Y.S.	say
	19/10/15		Routine as usual	say
	20/10/15		20 complete teams reported to L.O. 3rd Horse Dir. L6 Transport - for carrying return from Railhead to Reserve Park. 6 miles	say
	21/10/15		Capt- W.F.RIDER. proceeded on Special leave to U.K. 23/10/15 to 13/11/15 command of Company tended over to Lieut T.B.W.O.Gumpen	say

Army Form C. 2118.

WAR DIARY
3rd Cavalry Division
INTELLIGENCE SUMMARY. Auxiliary Horse Transport Co.

Map Reference Sheet 57c U.10 B.2.8

(Erase heading not required.)

Place	Date	Hour	Summary of Events and Information	Remarks and references to Appendices
Sheet 57c U.10 B.2.8	19/10/18		Railhead. E Transloy — 3 Sgts. 14 Teams & R'head for rations for Div. Troops.	
			7 L.D. horses (Remounts) from A.C. Details CLERY. D.1 T/4/2436 STONE J.P. from B.H.T.D. Routine as usual.	
	20/10/18		1 L.D. horse from D.A.C. K.H. taken on strength Asst. O.C.A.S.C. 2 Gfs + complete team (?) R'head for rations fr. (D.H.Q.) D.A.C.X C.H.C. Built 3 harness sheds.	
	23/10/18		T.3/S.R. 03128 Dr. LAINE A.J. evacuated 14 Aug & F.P. No.2 4 Teams for Camp Commandant. 2 fr. salvage (O.C.A.S.C) & 2 for events in charge & 8 for rations (D.H.Q.) D.A.C (C.H.C.) D'Tpe50 D'MUNGE taken over from D.A.P. Tanks Corps.	
	24/10/18		Inspection by G.O.C Div. in Dull order. Moved from LE MESNIL to ROCQUIGNY. ½ teams for Rations 1 Blacksy. for Work.	
	25/10/18		Railhead as before. Inspection by A.D.V.C. 2 L.D Horses 1 Mule evacuated. 12 Teams fr. Rations 2 Salvage. Routine & making Camp. K 13 M.V.S.	
	26/10/18		T:1/4253 Dr Murry S.L handed over to A.P.M. 2 wagons & Railhead	
	27/10/18		1 L.D. Horse evacuated to 13 M.V.S. D' Irena WILES from B.H.T.D.	
	28/10/18		Routine Full marching order parade by C.O. In need of rifle inspection	
	29/10/18		Dr Storey E. granted special leave to U.K	

WAR DIARY or INTELLIGENCE SUMMARY.

Army Form C. 2118.

Map Reference: 3rd Cavalry Division
Sheet 57c Aux. Horse Transport Coy.

Place	Date	Hour	Summary of Events and Information	Remarks and references to Appendices
Sheet 57c V.10 B.2.C.	30/10/18		Reached LE TRANSLOY. Routine as usual. Inspection by M.O.	
	31/10/18		do. Routine as usual.	

E. Dames-Longworth Lt.

No. 57th COMPANY. A.S.C.
No. 490
Date 31/10/18
3rd CAV. DIVISIONAL AUX. H.T.

Army Form C. 2118.

Map Reference   3rd Cavalry Division
Sheet 57c   Aunx H.T.C.
V.10 B.28   576 Company A.S.C.

WAR DIARY or INTELLIGENCE SUMMARY
(Erase heading not required.)

Place	Date	Hour	Summary of Events and Information	Remarks and references to Appendices
V.10 B.28	1/11/18		Railhead LE TRANSLOY 15 Teams E.10 R.H. for amn. 2 teams for Ordnance	E.D.P.
	2/11/18		do. 15 Teams do. do.	
	3/11/18		do. 15 do. do. do.	
	4/11/18		do. 15 do. do. do.	
	5/11/18		Routine as usual. Unser auth. O.C.A.S.C. 1 Team	
			1 wagon sent to each Regt. in Div. for amn + 1 to the H.Q. of	
			each Bryde. 1 extra wagon E.10 R.H.	
	6/11/18		Moved from ROCQUINY to INCHY-EN-ARTOIS.	E.D.P
	7/11/18		Moved to DOUAI	E.D.P
	8/11/18		Moved to WHTTISSRT 1 Mule died	E.D.P
	9/11/18		Railhead DON 14 Wagon S.P. from Rev. Park to be attached	E.D.P
			to Ammunition. M.T.G. delivered 2700 rounds 13pdr to	
			224 000 S.A.A. which was loaded on 22 wagons	
	10/11/18		do. Routine	E.D.P
	11/11/18		d. d.	E.D.P
	12/11/18		d. d.	E.D.P

Army Form C. 2118.

WAR DIARY 3rd Cav. Div. Amm. W.T. 576 Company A S C

or

INTELLIGENCE SUMMARY.

(Erase heading not required.)

Place	Date	Hour	Summary of Events and Information	Remarks and references to Appendices
Nattencourt	13/11/18		Marched to BURY	
BURY	14/11/18		At LILLE Ammunition handed over to M.T. Q	say
	15/11/18		do. Wagons & Can Bde & complete 13	
			Wagons & Can Bde. 1 to K Bty. (at present absent	say
			4 to 6th Bde. 1 to K Bty. (at present absent	
			1 to Div. H.Q. all for carrying stores Rays (arrht	
			No 2 M.W. & Tractors)	
			Administrative Orders	
	16/11/18		Surplus Motfork transferred to R.H. + R.F.A. dept. - 5 L.D. drivers received from	say
			Cav. Div. Reserve Park.	
	17/11/18		1 driver received from 3rd Cav. Div. R.P. - 1 wagon body, re handed to 3rd Cav. Div. R.P.	say
			Company moved from BURY to BASSILLY - 4 men granted leave to U.K.	
			Capt. W E. Ryder returned from leave	
	18/11/18		Company moved from BASSILLY to ENGLIEN - 3 L D personnel procured -	say
			3 O.R. reinforcements arrived	
	19/11/18		Lieut T.E.M.D. Simpson & 4 O.R. proceeded on leave to U.K. - 2 O.R. returned from 61/17 A.S.C	say
			2 O.R. returned from leave U.K. - 2 Officers horses Harness & Tank wagon procured Cont Reinforcements	
			Camp	

Army Form C. 2118.

WAR DIARY
or
INTELLIGENCE SUMMARY.

3rd Cavalry Division
Purchasing Horse Transport Company
576 Company A.S.C.

Map Reference: Brussels 98.6 / 1/100,000

(Erase heading not required.)

Instructions regarding War Diaries and Intelligence Summaries are contained in F. S. Regs., Part II. and the Staff Manual respectively. Title pages will be prepared in manuscript.

Place	Date	Hour	Summary of Events and Information	Remarks and references to Appendices
ENGLIEN	20/11/15		Company routine as usual – 1 L.D. leave from A.S.C. Headquarters received –	any
	21/11/15		Company moved from ENGLIEN to WATERLOO	any
WATERLOO	22/11/15		Company moved from WATERLOO to PERWEZ – good billets	any
PERWEZ	23/11/15		Sgt. Mr. Jackson returned from leave – routine as usual	any
	24/11/15		Company moved from PERWEZ to ODENGE	any
ODENGE	25/11/15		1 O.R. granted special leave to U.K. 25/11/15 to 7/12/15	any
	26/11/15		T/1/4258 Pte Runge A.L. referred to Company on completion of Sentence F.P.II. Company received 4 horses for issues on to 2nd Brigade	any
	27/11/15		Routine as usual.	any
	28/11/15		1 For Sgt & 4 O.R. granted leave to U.K. 30/11/15 to 14/12/15 – 1 O.R. returned from leave U.K. – 1 O.R. to Hospital	any
	29/11/15		Routine as usual – 80713856 Driver F. Horn awarded Allied medal (Posthumous) no	any
	30/11/15		1 O.R. returned from leave	any
			(a) This establishment of Company – 2 other ranks deficient – 2 Riding Horses surplus. Health of Company good – condition of Animals Harness & Transport good – to billets casualties during month – On detachment 3 Q. complete Journals	any

O.C. 3rd Cav. Divn. A.H.T.

WO 35

Auxiliary Horse Transport Coy. 3rd Cav. Div.

2/1/19

War Diary

December 1918

Army Form C. 2118

WAR DIARY *Auxiliary Horse Transport Company*
or
INTELLIGENCE SUMMARY   3rd Cavalry Division
576 Company R.A.S.C.

(Erase heading not required.)

Map Reference: BRUSSELS 1/100,000

Instructions regarding War Diaries and Intelligence Summaries are contained in F. S. Regs., Part II. and the Staff Manual respectively. Title pages will be prepared in manuscript.

Place	Date	Hour	Summary of Events and Information	Remarks and references to Appendices
ODENGE	1/12/18		At this date – Strength of Company – 2 other ranks deceased – 2 Riding Horses supplied	any
Nr. PERWEZ			Company on rest billets – Railhead – NAMUR – 1 O.R. admitted Hospital	
	2/12/18		1 O.R. admitted Hospital – 1 L.D. mule evacuated	any
	3/12/18		Lt. J.S.W.D. Simpson granted 7 days extension of leave	any
	4/12/18		Routine as usual	any
	5/12/18		do	any
	6/12/18		SS-12141 A/Sjt Siggers McIntosh G. A/C.Q. promoted to substantive rank. Authority A.C.I. 20/266 dated 29/11/18 – 1 O.R granted 14 days special leave to U.K. – 1 O.R. admitted to Hospital	any
	7/12/18		3 O.R.s granted leave 14 days to U.K.	any
	8/12/18		1 L.D. Horse died (on attachment)	any
	9/12/18		1 O.R. admitted to Hospital (sick on leave)	any
	10/12/18		Routine as usual	any
	11/12/18		do – 3 O.R.s granted 14 days leave to U.K.	any
	12/12/18		do	any
	13/12/18		do	any

WAR DIARY or INTELLIGENCE SUMMARY

Army Form C. 2118.

Auxiliary Horse Transport Company
3rd Cavalry Division
576 Company R.A.S.C.

Army Reference
BRUSSELS
1/100,000

Place	Date	Hour	Summary of Events and Information	Remarks and references to Appendices
ODENGE	14/12/18		Routine as usual. — 2 other ranks granted leave to U.K. (14 days)	
	15/12/18	Hrs 22	Company moved from ODENGE to BIENWART — 2 other ranks leave to U.K. (14 days)	
BIENWART	16/12/18		Company moved from BIENWART to MODAVE	
MODAVE	17/12/18		Company moved to lower end of MODAVE village to more convenient billets	
	18/12/18		Routine as usual	
	19/12/18		Hd. qrs. T.E.W.D. Bienwart personnel performed from here — 2 O.Rs attached to A.S.C. Headquarters now attached to Cav Corps Concentration Camp.	
	20/12/18		Routine as usual — 3 O.Rs leave to U.K. (14 days)	
	21/12/18		Routine as usual	
	22/12/18		4 complete forwards to ENGIS 4 reserve north they	
	23/12/18		do to TINLOT north they for reserve dumps required	
	24/12/18		6 other ranks dispatched to Concentration Camps SERAING for demobilization	
	25/12/18		6 other ranks leave to U.K. (14 days) 1 O.R. returned from leave	
	26/12/18		1 Craftsman to Con Camp SERAING for demobilization	
	27/12/18		Routine as usual	
	28/12/18		1 Craftsman to Con Camp SERAING for demobilization — 2 O.Rs returned leave	

Army Form C. 2118.

WAR DIARY
or
INTELLIGENCE SUMMARY.
(Erase heading not required.)

Auxiliary Horse Transport Company
3rd Cavalry Divisions
57th Company R.A.S.C.

Map Reference MARCHE 1/100,000

Place	Date	Hour	Summary of Events and Information	Remarks and references to Appendices
MODAVE	28/12/18		Routine as usual – 4 O.R. exchanged at L.S. Horse	nil
	29/12/18		1 L.D. here sent for Marches on detachment	nil
	30/12/18		1 O.R. admitted to Hospital – 3 Wagons 11 horses Thomas & 6 O.R. Transferred to Heavy Section Reserve Park. 3rd Cav. Div. them & replaced by Them exchanging 12 mules for 11 horses. Authority D.A.D.S.T. T. Army 1/use Q. Cav. Div. Copies 841/5. – 2 Conferences to be Comp – SERAING for demobilyation	nil
	31/12/18		Routine as usual At this date – Strength of Company – 1Y other ranks deficient – 2 L.D. Horses deficient – 2 Riding horses surplus – One detachment 35 complete. Turnouts – Health of Company good. – Condition of Animals Harness & good.	nil

W. Pitcher
Lieut.
O.C. 3rd Cav. Div. A.H.T.

AUXILIARY HORSE TRANSPORT COMPANY.

3RD CAVALRY DIVISION.

WAR DIARY.

JANUARY 1919.

WAR DIARY

Army Form C. 2118

3rd Cavalry Division — Auxiliary Horse Transport Company
576 Company R.A.S.C.

MARCHE INTELLIGENCE SUMMARY

Place	Date	Hour	Summary of Events and Information	Remarks and references to Appendices
MODAVE	1/1/19		At this date — strength of Company — 17 other ranks deprived — 2 L.D. horses deprived. — 2 Heavy Horse surplus — On detachment 39 complete turnouts. Routine as usual — 2 other ranks granted leave (14 days) to U.K.	
	2/1/19		1 L.D. horse cast for slaughter	any
	3/1/19		2 other ranks leave to U.K. (14 days)	any
	4/1/19		3 other ranks returned from leave U.K.	any
	5/1/19		3 other ranks reinforcements from B.H.T.D.	any
	6/1/19		1 other rank returned from leave U.K.	any
	7/1/19		Routine as usual	any
	8/1/19		do	any
	9/1/19		2 other ranks granted leave to U.K. (14 days)	any
	10/1/19		2 other ranks returned from leave U.K.	any
	11/1/19		1 other rank returned from leave U.K.	any
	12/1/19		1 other rank returned from Hospital. 1 other rank to Hospital. 11 other ranks proceeded on leave from Car Coys. Reinforcement Camp — overdue from leave	any
	13/1/19		4 other ranks attached turn to U.K. (14 days) Sergt / 2nd Lieut A.V.C. to SERAING for demobilisation	any

Army Form C. 2118.

WAR DIARY
or
INTELLIGENCE SUMMARY

Map Reference: 1/100,000
MARCHE

3rd Cavalry Division
Auxiliary Horse Transport Company
376 Company R.A.S.C.

(Erase heading not required.)

Place	Date	Hour	Summary of Events and Information	Remarks and references to Appendices
MODAVE	14/1/19		1 mule evacuated - 4 reinforcements arrived from B.H.T.D.	ang
	15/1/19		Routine as usual	ang
	16/1/19		do. 6 other ranks granted leave (14 days) to U.K. - 1 O.R. to	ang
			SERAING for demobilization (coal miner)	
	17/1/19		Routine as usual	ang
	18/1/19		1 L.D. horse evacuated. 1 mule evacuated	ang
	19/1/19		Routine as usual	ang
	20/1/19		6 other ranks granted leave (14 days) to U.K.	ang
	21/1/19		Routine as usual	ang
	22/1/19		do	ang
	23/1/19		do	ang
	24/1/19		1 large Maggs Ford. sundry German stores &c collected & sent to Adv. Depot	ang
	25/1/19		3 Other ranks granted leave to U.K. 14 days. 169 personnel from Corps H.Q. The following complete turnout returned from detachment. 6th Brigade 3 - 7th Brigade 7 - one	ang
			mule evacuated	
	26/1/19		2 other ranks to SERAING for demobilization. 1 O.R. admitted Hospital	ang

Army Form C. 2118.

WAR DIARY
or
INTELLIGENCE SUMMARY

Troop Reference: 3rd Cavalry Division
Auxiliary Horse Transport Company
57th Company – R.A.S.C.

(Erase heading not required.)

Instructions regarding War Diaries and Intelligence Summaries are contained in F. S. Regs., Part II. and the Staff Manual respectively. Title pages will be prepared in manuscript.

Place	Date	Hour	Summary of Events and Information	Remarks and references to Appendices
MODAVE	27/1/19		1 O.R. admitted to Hospital, 1 O.R. reinforcement arrived from B.H.T.D.	
	28/1/19		Good cat on detachment, 9 complete turnouts to 7th Cavalry Brigade.	
	29/1/19		4 O.Rs. granted leave to U.K. (14 days)	
	30/1/19		1 O.R. granted special leave to U.K. (14 days) Routine as usual	
	31/1/19		(1) this date — Strength of Company — 19 other ranks deployed – 5 L.D. Horses acquired – 2 Riding horses employed – On detachment 36 complete turnouts. Health of Company good – condition of Horses Harness Equipment & good	

W. Fisher
Capt.
O.C. 3rd Cav. Div. A.H.T.

WAR DIARY
or
INTELLIGENCE SUMMARY
(Erase heading not required.)

Army Form C. 2118.

Army Reference: 3rd Cavalry Division
Auxiliary Horse Transport Company
576 Company R.A.S.C.   AHC 39

Place	Date	Hour	Summary of Events and Information	Remarks and references to Appendices
MODAVE	1/2/19		At this date - Strength of Company - 19 Other ranks absent - 5 L.D. Horses deficient - 1/2 Relay Horse surplus - On detachment 36 - complete Turnouts -	
	2/2/19		Routine as usual. - 1 complete Turnout for Reserves TINLOT.	nil
	3/2/19		do do	nil
	4/2/19		do do	nil
	5/2/19		1 Farrier Serg.t + 2 O.R. + 1 complete Turnout to Cav. bde Annual Gathering Camp ENGHIS	nil
	6/2/19		1 L.D. Horse + 1 Mule evacuated to British Veterinary Section	nil
	7/2/19		All animals (L.D) at Company Headquarters examined by Remount + Veterinary Board - 2 B.R.c. turn to W.R (in dep.) - 1 O.R. to Cav. bde Concentration Camp for demobilization - 1 L.S. Wagon and 1 O.R. + H.L.D. Horses removed thereto thereto H.L.D	nil
	8/2/19		1 O.R. to Cav. bde Concentration Camp for demobilization - 2 L.S. Wagons + demob.g groups 4 L.D. Horses + 4 Mules with Harness complete to Cav. Bde 2nd Horse depot SERAING for duty. Authority: O.C. RASC. - 1 D.R. to Concentration Camp - SERAING for demobilization	nil
	9/2/19		All animals at H.Q.rs of Unit (HT) inspected by V.O. - O.C. attended Court of Enquiry at ENGHIS	nil
	10/2/19		Routine as usual -	nil

WAR DIARY / INTELLIGENCE SUMMARY

Army Form C. 2118.

Map Reference: 3rd Cav. Bde. Am. M.T.C.
MARCHE
676 Company R.A.S.C.
Movers

Place	Date	Hour	Summary of Events and Information	Remarks and references to Appendices
MODAYE	11/2/19		Routine as usual —	E.D.P.
	12/2/19		1 Man to collecting camp ENG15. 1 L.D. deputated from C.Batt. to ENG15	E.D.P.
			1 Sgt. from 8 H.T.D. reported for duty	E.D.P.
			Capt. RYDER having proceeded on leave to U.K. LT E. DAWES SIMPSON takes over command from this day.	E.D.P.
	13/2/19		Sgt. TRIBE to H.Q. CAN. CAV. BDE	E.D.P.
	14/2/19		Routine as usual —	E.D.P.
	15/2/19		Cas'y horses to collecting camp ENG16	E.D.P.
	16/2/19		Routine as usual	
	17/2/19		6 Z L.D. horses to PERAINE. 1 L.D. to Can A.M.V.S.	E.D.P.
			Capt. Whalen CLARKE & Dv. Whalen (left for duty 14 VIII M. L.C.C. ENG15 from 1st R.DF.S. 15-2-19	E.D.P.
			Routine as usual	E.D.P.
	18/2/19		4 L.D. horses Z. from 10 R. Hussars & Z. cont 18-2-19	E.D.P.
	19/2/19		1 Mule No. 63 case from A. Batt. to 4th Can M.V.S. 9-2-19	E.D.P.
			3 L.D. horses Z from 1st R.D.L.Z. depot 18-2-19	E.D.P.
			All horses returned to H.Q. under instruction from "Q"	E.D.P.

WAR DIARY
INTELLIGENCE SUMMARY. 676 Company R.A.S.C.

Army Form C. 2118.

3rd Can. Div. A.H.T.C.

Map Reference MARCHE

Place	Date	Hour	Summary of Events and Information	Remarks and references to Appendices
MODAVE	22/2/19	1/00 ans	1 L.D. Horse "Y" dispatched from Escort Sqdn X R.H. & A.S.C. ENGIS.	S.O.S
	21/2/19		Dr. WHITEHEAD 22050 R.F.A. & Dr. METCALFE 12409 R.F.A. & Great Cny	S.O.S
	22/2/19		Routine as usual	S.O.S
	23/2/19		do	S.O.S
	24/2/19		7 L.D. Horses Y to C.C. General Collec. Camp 1 L.D.H. "D" & Can. M.V.S.	S.O.S
	25/2/19		Routine as usual	
	26/2/19		Dr. DOYLE 6496 R.F.A. & CONCERT for demobilisation	S.O.S
	27/2/19		Routine as usual	
	28/2/19		3 Riders 3 L.D. Horses "Z" with ar HUY.	
			5 Riders 4 L.D.H. Z L Z. Dpot Boning. 2 L.D. Horses fm. Fy. Sqdn	S.O.S
			6 Z. Horses Dpot SERAING	

E. Dawes /mjsr

Barnes Lt Can B14 A.H.T.

WAR DIARY or INTELLIGENCE SUMMARY.

Army Form C. 2118.

Auxiliary Horse Transport Company
3rd Cavalry Division
57th Company R.A.S.C.

Map Reference MARCHE 1/100,000

Place	Date	Hour	Summary of Events and Information	Remarks and references to Appendices
MODAVE Sq HQy	1/3/19		On this date, strength of Company:- 31 O.R's deficient.- 1 Saddler surplus.	
			19 L.D animals surplus - deficient 1 R. Horse. On detachment	
			1 Farrier! - 1 Wheeler Corpl - 1 Corpl - 12 O.R - 20 animals +	
			5 G.S waggons with Harness complete	207
			1 L.D Mule draught - 34 Z Mules to 3rd Cav Div R.P. - 3 R.	
	2/3/19		Horses 1 L.D Horse 110 Mules (X) from 3rd Cav Div R.P.	207
			1 O.R rank S/S Mchy Spark M'Graph deploaned	
	3/3/19		1 G.S waggon drivers from Harness complete to A.C.C ENGIS	
			1 do do " Concent SERAING	207
			2 do do " "Z" Horse Depot SERAING	
			Capt. M.E RIDER returned from leave & took over command of Company	
	4/3/19		1 O.R. referred from Hospital. 14 Unbranded animals marked by A.D.V.S	207
	5/3/19		1 L.D. to 13 R. M.V.S. for destruction	
			4 L.D Horses "Z" + 3 Mules "Z" transferred to 3rd Cav Div R.P. - 1 R. Horse received	207
			on loan from R.A.S.C. Headquarters	
	6/3/19		Company moved to CLERMONT nr ENGIS nr LIEGE 1/100,000	204

Army Form C. 2118.

Auxiliary Horse Transport Company
3rd Cavalry Division
576 Company R.A.S.C.

WAR DIARY or INTELLIGENCE SUMMARY.

(Erase heading not required.)

Map Reference
LIEGE
1/100,000

Instructions regarding War Diaries and Intelligence Summaries are contained in F. S. Regs., Part II. and the Staff Manual respectively. Title pages will be prepared in manuscript.

Place	Date	Hour	Summary of Events and Information	Remarks and references to Appendices
CLERMONT	7/3/19		Rations drawn by Horse Transport from Railhead - ENGIS	
" ENGIS	6/3/19		1/Corpl Budd E. to SERAING for demobilization	
	9/3/19		1 L.D. Horse evacuated to 15th M.V.S. - The undermentioned wounded personnel were despatched under instructions R.A.S.C.	
			3 teams complete with Harness to 4th Bde R.H.A. (1 Corpl i/c charge of each party)	
			28 pairs wheelers complete with Harness to 3rd Cav DAC	
			1 G.S. waggon with team, Driver Harness to 165.69 (P.O.W.)	
			1 O.R. to C.C.A Gallophy Camp ENGIS for duty as clerk	
			Corpl McDougall R. to Hospital - (Ebury Horse Artillery returned from Div Hqrs?)	
	10/3/19		1 O.R. granted leave of absence to U.K. (14 days)	
	11/3/19		Farr. Sgt. Brown & Sr. DIXON from an O.C. ENGIS	
	12/3/19		Capt W.E. RIDER & C.C. PERMIT for demobilization 11 'X' Mule from Rail	
	13/3/19		1 Cpl from Hospital 1 P.L.D. 1 Sgt & 1 R.L. & O.C. 10th Hussars & escort in move the party to report to O.C. 4th Hussars for move to AMAY	8/S.P
	14/3/19		1 L.D. Horse & 13th M.V.S.	
	15/3/19		41 L.D. & Sgt report to O.C. 4th Hussars for move Cpl. & 1 O.R. & C.C. SERAING	

Map Reference

WAR DIARY Auxiliary Horse Transport C Army Form C. 2118.

LIÈGE INTELLIGENCE SUMMARY. 9th Cavalry Division

57 C. R.A.S.C.

1/100,000

(Erase heading not required.)

Place	Date	Hour	Summary of Events and Information	Remarks and references to Appendices
CLERMONT	16/3/19		Routine as usual	EDS
	17/3/19		2 L.D. horses to 2nd D. mules to Z depot Liney	EDS
	18/3/19		2 drivers transferred to 1st Cav. Div.	EDS
	19/3/19		4 drivers 12 mules 2 G.S. wagons agreed D.S. from 10th Hussars	EDS
	20/3/19		6 n per horse sent to 3rd Field Squadron to move nags to Park	EDS
	21/3/19		1 L.D. Horse 11 mule to 13th M.V.S.	EDS
	22/3/19		D'ENGLES & D'LAINE to CONCENT SERAINE	EDS
	23/3/19		4 Mules transferred from H.Q. R.A.S.C. to the unit	EDS
	24/3/19		9 drivers transferred from H.Q. R.A.S.C.	EDS
	24/3/19		10 Tagman to Hospital	EDS
	25/3/19		1 L.D. Mule No 79 to 13 M.V.S.	EDS
	26/3/19		15 from to PLATINAGE to escort 11th Hussars Entrainment	EDS
			20 from to CHOKIER to escort "K" Battery Entrainment	EDS

Map Reference: Auxiliary Horse Transport 1st Cav. Div.
WAR DIARY / INTELLIGENCE SUMMARY. 3rd Cav. Div.
LIE & E   576 C RASC
1/100 000

Place	Date	Hour	Summary of Events and Information	Remarks and references to Appendices
CLERMONT	27/3/19		Routine as usual	ELD
	28/3/19		do	ELD
	29/3/19		2/Lt RICKETT & CONCENT CAMP	PLD
	2/3/19		7 Drivers (veterans) transferred to 1st Cav. Div.	
			7 x Riders to SENT to 1st Div.	ELD
	31/3/19		Routine as usual.	

E Dawson Simpson
Comdg. 3rd Cav. Div. A.H.T.C.

WAR DIARY or INTELLIGENCE SUMMARY

Army Form C. 2118

Map Reference: LIEGE 1/100,000

Auxiliary Horse Transport Co.
3rd Cavalry Division
576 Company A.S.C.

WC 39

Place	Date	Hour	Summary of Events and Information	Remarks and references to Appendices
CLERMONT	Apl 1st		4 L.D. Mules to A.C.C. ENGIS	
	2nd		7 horses 16 Mules 4 wagons rejoined company from Z Res dept SERAING	
	3rd		4 L.D. Mules from A.C.C. ENGIS to Z dept SERAING	
	4th		Routine as usual	
	5th		do.	
	6th		All animals of Company (192) to A.C.C. ENGIS	
			80 L.D. mules from 2nd A.H.T. joined	
	7th		All vehicles & saddlery handed in to DADOS	
	8th		20 pairs complete to 1st Cav Res Park	
	9th		Moved to JEMMEPPE	
JEMMEPPE	Apl 10th		Routine as usual	
	11th		do	
	12th		2 N.C.O's 20 pairs mules to 3rd Cav Div Res Park	
	13th		Nil	
	14th		20 pairs to Res Park 3rd Div. for entrainment	
	15th		3 pairs to A.C.C. ENGIS. 12 men to CONCENT CAMP.	

Map Reference LIEGE

WAR DIARY 3rd Cav. Bri. A.H.T.C.
INTELLIGENCE SUMMARY 576 Company R.A.S.C.
1/1 in 1 m

Place	Date	Hour	Summary of Events and Information	Remarks and references to Appendices
JEMEPPE	Apr 16th		Nil	
	17th		14 pair to 7th Cav. F.A. for removal of vehicles	
	18th		Nil	
	19th		do	
	20th		1 O.R. to Hospital	
	21st		1 O.R. to Hospital	
	22nd		Nil	
	23rd		13 pair & 1 single mule to move 4th Division from AMAY. 20 mules to CONCENT	
	24th		4 pair to 14th M.V.S. 10 team 2 pair, 1 single mule to C.R.H.A.	
	25th		3 team 3 pair to D.R. Cable Section. 1 team 16 pair to 7th M.G.C.	
	26th		17 pair to 6th M.G.S. to assist in entrainment.	
	27th		10 pair to DADOS. 7 mules to CONCENT CAMP.	
	28th		Nil	
	29th		"	
	30		"	

E Danver Simpson Lt.
O/C 3rd Cav. Div. A.H.T.C.

Army Form C. 2118.

WAR DIARY
or
INTELLIGENCE SUMMARY.
(Erase heading not required.)

Army Troop MGC? Edge

AMT Coy
2nd Cav Div
1/1917
6th Cav Bde B.E.F.

Instructions regarding War Diaries and Intelligence Summaries are contained in F. S. Regs., Part II. and the Staff Manual respectively. Title pages will be prepared in manuscript.

Place	Date	Hour	Summary of Events and Information	Remarks and references to Appendices
REMI SPE	17 May		W. E. ELLIMPSON proceeded on leave to UK	
	18	"	NIL	
	19	"	NIL	
	20	"	NIL	
	21	"	NIL	
	22	"	NIL	
	23	"	NIL	
	24	"	NIL	
	25	"	NIL	
	26	"	61167 Mulro to BonRemont Squadron	
			Transf. to 2nd Cav Div MMT Coy. 1707 B Officers	
	27	"	40 Pets Rations dispatched	PEPPINGER
	28	"	Company orders dispatched	to UK Wounded
	29	"	Company closed down.	

W. Townshill
Capt
OC 2nd Cav Div AMT Co.

W. E. ELLIMPSON
6 UK 14 days
on end

181 40

Map Reference
1/E 25

WAR DIARY
or
INTELLIGENCE SUMMARY.

Army Form C. 2118.

O.N.T.C. 2nd Can. Div. —
576 Company R.E.& C.

Instructions regarding War Diaries and Intelligence Summaries are contained in F. S. Regs., Part II. and the Staff Manual respectively. Title pages will be prepared in manuscript.

(Erase heading not required.)

Place	Date	Hour	Summary of Events and Information	Remarks and references to Appendices
JEMIMEPPE	May 1st		1 H.T. Driver to CONCENT.	
	2nd		do	
	3rd		nil	
	4th		nil	
	5th		nil	
	6th		nil	
	7th		nil	
	8th		1 N.C.O. 6 O.R. to CONCENT for demobilisation	
	9th		1 O.R. to hospital	
	10th		nil	
	11th		10 O.R. leave to U.K.	
	12th		19 L.D. Medico to No.11 General Squadron JEMBES	
	13th		NIL	
	14th		NIL	
	15th		NIL	
	16th		Capt. J. NESBITT McILL R.E.C. takes over command vice V/LT SIMPSON leave to U.K.	

www.ingramcontent.com/pod-product-compliance
Lightning Source LLC
Chambersburg PA
CBHW081536160426
43191CB00011B/1770